COMMUNITY AND UNITY

COMMUNITY AND UNITY

Basil Al-Bayati

ACADEMY EDITIONS · LONDON/ST. MARTIN'S PRESS · NEW YORK

First published in Great Britain in 1983 by
Academy Editions 7/8 Holland Street London W8

Published in the United States of America in 1983 by
St. Martin's Press 175 Fifth Avenue New York NY 10010

ISBN 0-312-15298-1

Printed and bound in Hong Kong

Basil Al-Bayati

BASIL AL-BAYATI is an architect who has a special interest in the concept of unity, appropriate to the design of modern cities for the Arab world. *Community and Unity* is but one of his many large-scale projects which incorporate his forward-looking ideas. His extensive knowledge of traditional Islamic culture, together with his talents as a planner, have enabled him to put into practice what must surely be essential to any design for a Middle Eastern community. The author sees a sensitive understanding of the Islamic heritage with regard to human scale, combined with an awareness of contemporary needs within the community as especially important to planning. The result is a humanistic, yet exciting approach to design. Basil Al-Bayati was trained at the University of Baghdad, University College, London and the Architectural Association in London. He is a member of many professional bodies and currently works both in the Middle East and United Kingdom. His work was on exhibition at the Venice Biennale (1982) and this book is just one of several publications by the author, among which is *Process and Pattern*, published in 1981.

Contents

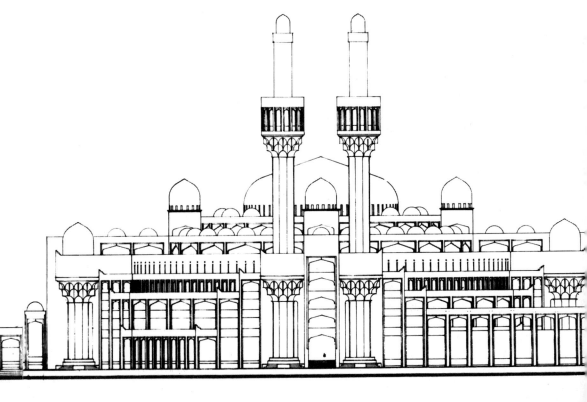

Preface

Several approaches to the urban problems of Arab cities were presented and discussed in the symposium on 'The Arab City: its Character and Islamic Cultural Heritage', held in Medina during February and March 1981. There, it was emphasized that most solutions following the Western model of urbanization are lacking when applied to Arab cities.

The question is whether Arab planners and architects should keep following ideas that were created for the countries where they originated or whether they should try to develop their own original paths. I am personally one of the exponents of the original paths.

I have recently come across one example of the ingenious solution to the Arab urban structure which was created by Basil Al-Bayati as a design for a new residential and commercial complex for Abu Dhabi. His design is based on the concept of unity in planning in accordance with the rule of the Divine Law.

This architect is a newcomer to Arab architecture. His scheme shows a great architectural and planning talent. Behind it is a great philosophical concept.

The architecture and planning of Mr Al-Bayati's scheme challenges the style of the architecture of the Modern Movement which has been used to design Arab cities in the last decade.

One can see clearly in the planning of the whole project the relation of his architecture to the great architecture of the Islamic world in the past, with its religious, social and political aspects. He succeeds in adapting this to the present technology in an ingenious way. A strong image of Islamic architectural tradition dominates the entire project; indeed, looking at the design of the complex one notices a monumental scale. His architecture is grand and yet it is very easy to construct, as it is based on prefabricated units, which make it economically viable.

The spread of Islam from its beginning in the seventh century was very rapid and within a century the Muslim dominion extended to vast areas of the world. During that period they developed a magnificent original architecture.

Basil Al-Bayati said to me *'I believe in making use of the examples of the thousands of years of Islamic heritage. I am trying to learn our heritage from our history and trying to bring it back today, as it has almost been forgotten.'*

His planning ideas were based upon using the geometric discipline used in most Islamic cities, the buildings within the city and details of elements within these buildings. The basic idea of the planning of this scheme came from the concept of a linear, covered walkway, which appeared in the old bazaars of Islamic cities; the other planning basis was the open courtyard which recalls the Mosques, palaces, Madrassas. The covered walkway and the courtyard are basic elements of the design. Others, such as high walls, domes, wind towers, pools and intermediate spaces, give the scheme a thread of communication with the past architecture of the Islamic world. The traditional order extends even into the design of the gardens within the courtyards. Great effort was put into the choice of the elements of Grand Islamic architecture for the new design, in order to find a solution which corresponds to the past and yet represents the present.

The exterior form of the facade forms the interior element of the space; circular columns house the staircase, bathroom or sometimes the living space. The construction method suggested in the design was chosen to meet the needs of the building and system module, to ease and speed construction.

It is essential to link the development concept with the traditional concept of the past.

Only by understanding the society and carefully examining its roots can we understand the nature and the values of its architectural and urban heritage. Basil Al-Bayati's goal is to revive the architecture of Islam.

His work shows that the future of architecture for the Islamic world lies in a return to a new concept of understanding of the architecture of the past.

I am sure his architecture and planning ideas will produce a reaction in the present and future generations of the Islamic world.

Dr Mohamed A. Al Hammad
Director General
Arab Urban Development Institute

Introduction

Following the completion of my paper *Community and Unity*, in which I discussed the concept of unity in Islam in relation to its urban structures, it occurred to me to elucidate my ideas through a partial design. Happily this coincided with the announcement of a competition for the design of a multi-functional residential and commercial centre in one of the Arab cities set up by the Department of Social Services and Commercial Buildings Administration. I have always felt that the concept of unity was particularly suited to the design of modern-day cities in the Islamic/Arabic world, and this concern has naturally been supported by my national and cultural involvement with this part of the world, together with my knowledge of modern technology, gained through work experience both in the Middle East and the West.

Feeling this competition to be of practical benefit to my ideas, I contacted a friend of mine who has a local consultants' firm, and as a result I formed a consortium of professional bodies, with myself as the architectural designer and planner. We were invited to submit our design for the competition, the subject of which was given on pages 3 and 9 of the brief sent to me:

(3)

'The aim of this competition is to obtain the best designs for a residential and commercial complex within the city centre, which will include all its complementary services within an integrated framework. Consideration should be paid to the many social and economic objectives which will positively affect the city and its citizens.'

(9)

'The design of the proposed complex on the six zones should include many elements which would complement each other both functionally and visually, within a balanced framework of economical, social and environmental considerations.

'These elements are:
C/1—Housing
C/2—Offices
C/3—Commercial and shopping
C/4—Recreational
C/5—Car Parking.'

The project entailed two discouraging factors. Primarily, the design was for one particular part of the city, the shape of which was fixed as six linear zones; likewise, the principal vehicular system was also already established. Secondly, the time factor was extremely limiting with only three months in which to complete the design—a difficult task considering the area of the site (in this case, 360,000 m^2)—and, of course, it was necessary to study the density of such an area in order to achieve an environmentally balanced project. However, there were many encouraging points, as indicated on page 8 of the brief:

(8)

'Consideration must be given to the architectural concepts of both the project as a whole, and to its individual elements, bearing in mind the size and the multi-functional nature of the project. This should be in accordance with the desire of adopting higher architectural standards, inspired by the inherited cultural values of the area, which form part of the Arab Islamic heritage.'

In the last symposium held at Medina, ('The Arab City: its Character and Islamic Cultural Heritage', February-March 1981), in which I participated, I remember how my friend encouraged me to feel that it is our historic duty as members of that part of the world, to concern ourselves with the future state of our cities. We should not stand still and watch their deterioration, but should act positively towards producing a feasible solution. In spite of the difficulties involved, I was encouraged to proceed with the scheme, and consequently called all the other parties together for a meeting. After only five days, I had established an idea for a design, incorporating my concept of unity in the Islamic community, and within the following two weeks, production and drawings began.

My idea for the design originated from two factors. Firstly, the **courtyard** and covered market within the residential and commercial zones would act as a link to all parts of the community. This stemmed from the original planning of the Islamic culture, and fitted with the brief of the competition, page 16:

(16)

'D/I Pedestrian Movement
Which is in two main parts:
—Movement outside the perimeter of the project, which should be in compliance with the area's pattern. Special emphasis to be given to the main approaches, through material, colour and area.
—Movement within the project. The designer should consider the areas and widths of the main and secondary alleys and pathways, which should serve the community in a convenient and smooth manner, through variation and appealing shading (either by use of sheds, or within buildings, protected by overhangings, or within spaces . . .)'

The vehicular and pedestrian system was designed on the basis of a gradation in scale of movement, in order to achieve a balance between modern-day requirements and consideration for the human environment, characteristic of the old Islamic city. This likewise fitted with the brief of the competition, page 15:

(15)

'Traffic should be restricted to the main and secondary roads, with preferably, the exits and entrances of the parking areas confined to the secondary roads, to avoid any proximity. However, consideration should be given to the location of better spaces on the main roads, for the purposes of economic activities. Consideration for pedestrian movement is required.'

The covered and semi-covered walkways, characteristic of the old Islamic environment, provided a solution to the climatic problems, as required in the brief, page 19:

(19)

'The designer is asked to consider the architectural expansion of the environment and to make use of natural ventilation and proper air movements, together with the study of the solar angles, and the impact these factors will have on the human environment.

'Because of the significant location of the project zones, placed within the city's central area, and in accordance with the multi-functional nature of the complex, the designer is required to consider the importance of the visual organization of the project as a whole including its individual elements. However, the architectural details should reflect the Arab Islamic heritage, placed in a contemporary image and not necessarily deviating from traditional "stages".'

The other important element was the Mosque. It was located in such a way as to act as a central unit, around which all other activities could grow. This was also discussed in the brief, under 'Complementary services to the Housing', page 11:

(11)
'Mosques
The existing mosques will be checked. The number of those proposed for the inhabitants, will bear reference to the housing capacity of the project.'

The height of the centre was carefully considered in the design. It would have been preferable to keep the height to a minimum, but taking into account the requirements of the brief (page 10), such height has been confined to office space.

(10)

'The designer will consider the required density, in order to provide adequate and efficient services, and balance within the open spaces, bearing in mind that in some cases, the height of the residential towers will not exceed from 15 to 20 floors.'

Consideration in the design was paid to the social behaviour of the people who live according to the Divine Law. Private and public spaces were also considered carefully, as required by the brief (page 18).

(18)

'In order to create a civilized expression for the city within the Arab Islamic framework, the project will provide all the necessary modern-day facilities. The designer is also reminded of the particular population composition of the city and the area, and of the consequent factors—as follows:

'Consideration should be given to the activities where segregation between the sexes is still respected, in accordance with valid social values. Provision of multi-accesses may be required in some parts, for both men and women.'

As specified in the brief (page 19), I have regarded the visual and aesthetic aspects of the design as important factors. Naturally, the scale was a problem, but I have incorporated the use of **gateways** to allow for access, and similarly, the column, which is suggestive of strength, was constructed on a different scale to take a stairway or lift. Likewise, I have used the **patio** to provide an intermediate space. The use of the gateway helps divide the urban structure into different sections, and acts as a unifying element within the design, as does the circle—used in the design of openings. At one time, domes played an important part in representing unity of space. Consequently, the presence of light within domes and other spaces has helped to unify both the interiors and exteriors. The wind tower has incorporated all these elements and, of course, acts as a true reflection of the Arab Islamic heritage.

The planning of the scheme is based on the principle of unity—the whole being made up of cellular units. These cellular units contain courtyards and covered walkways. Each unit is connected to the other, by covered walkways. The connection is made in such a way that the addition of secondary units will create further secondary courtyards.

The cellular units are composed of smaller segments of equal form—each accommodating different functions. In order to achieve variety, as specified in the brief (page 12), each segment is capable of changing in size.

(12)
'Flexibility is a major feature, and should be incorporated into the design.'

The concept of unity within the design is explained in the following pages of this book, together with the project itself, and many illustrations and drawings. As this proposal concerns the people of Islamic countries, I hope the time will come when they themselves will read and judge it. In the meantime, I must address it to those people responsible for creating such environments—to the architects, the planners, the sociologists and to the regional and international officials whose problem it is to organize the Arab cities. I would like to make a grateful acknowledgement to all those who have helped to produce this scheme, and I give heartfelt thanks for the many candles burnt at both ends, by all concerned—the end has justified the means.

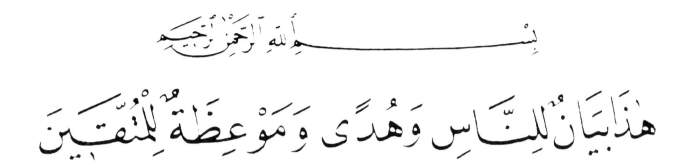

'This is a declaration for mankind, a guidance and instruction to those who fear God.'

Quran (Al-Imran 3:138)

Purpose

During the twentieth century the Islamic Arab city has lost some of its original character. This is because of the introduction of foreign values and foreign architectural ideas. **It is our responsibility at the present time to try and prevent this continuing.**

The aim is to design the project on the basis of the implementation of Islamic beliefs. We have avoided using the previous method because of the rapid development in Arab countries. This method came out of a strange phenomenon: that of the simplification of traditional architecture and the addition of some traditional elements such as arches. This method was employed without any deep understanding of the cultural values of Islamic civilization.

Source

The source of architecture and planning in the Islamic world does not follow any theory or philosophy or methodology, nor does it follow any system of proportion, shape or form of building. It is not an expression of any past or present technology, neither is it a particular kind of door or window, arch, dome or minaret.

It is architecture created by man's concern for the Divine Law (*shariah*) and his behaviour according to it within the Islamic society. **It is architecture concerned with unity**, built by people who have Islamic faith. It is what I call '*polite*' architecture.

Environment

'Wa'btaghi fi ma ataka'l-Lahu'd dara'l akhirata wa la tansa naṣibaka mina'd dunyā was aḥsin kama ahsana'l lahū 'ilaika wa la tabghi'l fasada fi'l arḍi. Innua'l-Laha la yuḥibbu'l mufsidin.'

Hadith Sharif

'Life can only be understood backwards; but it must be lived forwards.'

Soren Kierkegaard

Architectural space in the Islamic world is very original. It was born with Islam and developed from religious, social, political and geographical factors. **Out of religion the open courtyard emerged** along with the Iwan. As for the social factors, these affected the development of the Islamic Arab architecture which can be seen in the **covered market which links up all parts of the community.** As for political factors, these had a strong influence on the architectural walls and towers, and high fences appeared as a result. The geographical factors had an even greater effect, since the location, the atmospheric state, and the geological foundations have all affected Islamic architecture.

Architectural spaces such as courtyards, covered markets, high walls and inward planning are all essential in the planning of the new urban structure.

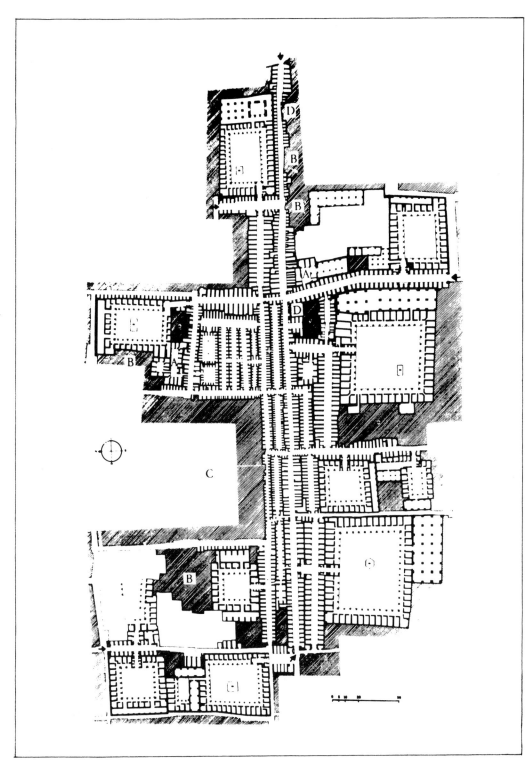

Souq, each devoted to a separate trade, with Mosque, Madrassa and Khans—Ottoman Period

Covered Souq from the late Islamic Period

Courtyard

'Wa jannatin 'arḍuha's samawatū wa'l arḍ.'
(A paradise that has the space of heaven and earth.)

Quran (3:133)

'Jamāhika ya wajha'l-fadā'i 'ajibu
wa sadruka ya'ba'l-intihā'a rahību.'
(Your beauty, O face of the space is wonderful,
And your chest is so fast as to challenge limitation.)

Rusafi

Sahan consists of an open space surrounded by a building. This principle of planning gives the building sufficient illumination, the requisite ventilation and acts as a sieve to purify the air from all dust particles. It also cuts noise down from adjoining roads. It traps warmth in winter and lowers the temperature of intense heat in the summer. For social and religious purposes it helps to achieve privacy. It is a place where trees and flowers are planted and fountains are located.

The open courtyard is still considered to be the most convenient of all designs to serve these purposes. So it can be used in today's planning of Arab cities. **The open courtyard presents the first concept of unity in space. It has been used in Mosques, hotels, schools, hospitals and palaces.**

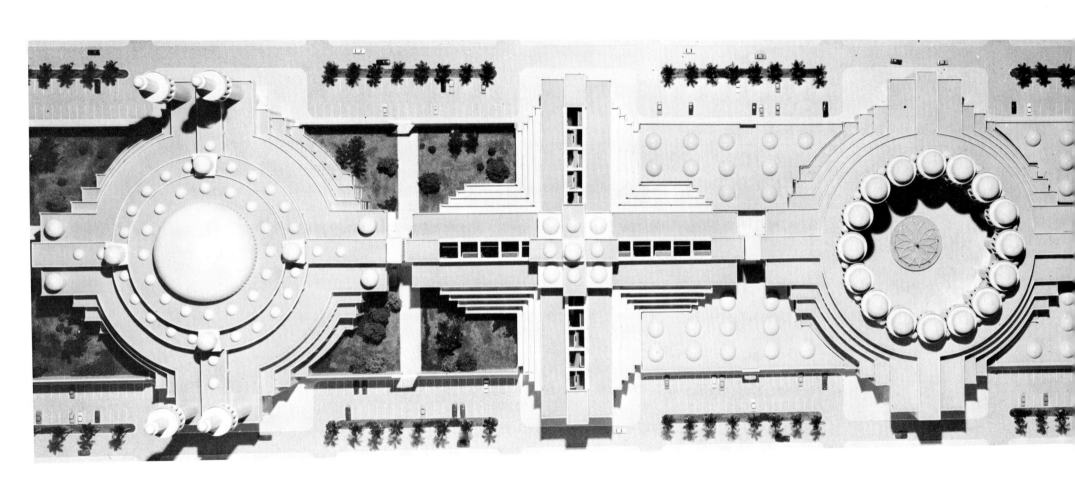

Market

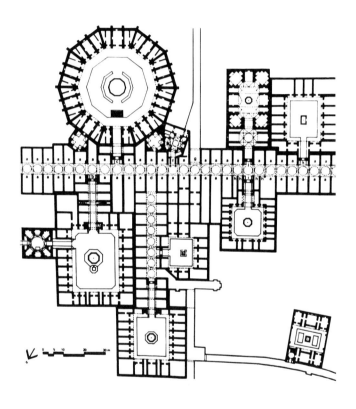

One of the easiest ways of finding out about the contemporary Islamic Arab City with its cultural entity is at the commercial markets known as *bazaars* or *souqs*. These were one of the commonest features of the Islamic City, and had a type of planning which can be used today to stimulate social relations amongst the flow of people and also to encourage the commercial movement of surrounding trading centres. The longitudinal planning for distribution services in the residential areas is a unifying element. The souq can be used to link all the other activities surrounding it and can operate as a service element. **The purpose of such a link is to make the whole community one unit.**

The First

The number 'one' is the principal and origin of all numbers. When one talks of geometry, it represents the centre; whilst in terms of space it is representative of one departure point from its source. In terms of measurement, it indicates the quantitative space between two points; and when one considers direction it represents the one point moving away from its original position. This movement produces a line-path and the movement of that path when the origin is fixed forms the arch, symbolizing the origin (one) as the controlling element. This control achieves an enclosed circle and once this is completed a unity is obtained. **The circle indicates equality from the centre.**

Ahad means unity.

There is no God, but God and Mohammed is the prophet of God (*ta illaha illa llah, Mohammed rasula llah*). This expresses the multiplicity of form in relation to unity. To recognize the origin as a base of multiplicities of all forms shows us the straight way. There is always a relationship with the origin. It is the straight pathway.

'God "There is no God but the living the self-subsisting eternal"'.

'God doth belong to the dominion of the heavens and the earth and all that is therein.'

'Everything belongs to God [Ahad].'

The contact of the individual with the divine principle is the centre of consciousness. This is also represented by the spirit, which is, in this case, the secret [sir] controlling all forms which belong to God.

'The God of you all is to God.'

The meaning of the unity of being is to realize that one was never separate from God.

The Sura of True Faith

'In the name of God, the merciful one, say:
"God is one God, the eternal God; He begeteth not, neither is He begotten: and
there is not anyone like unto Him".'

Quran (62:1–3)

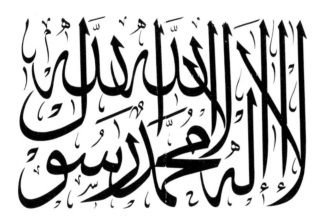

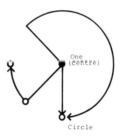

The First and The Last

The first odd number is one. The second odd number is three. When three circles come to rest with their outermost points just touching, the triangle is established. The triangle indicates the minimal expression of an area. These adjoining circles can be repeated to achieve a pattern which represents unity. Seven circles complete a hexagon, so from the principle of unity the first is the circle; the second is the triangle and the third is the hexagon. The square emerges as a product of this basic pattern. The equilateral triangle, the hexagon and the square are three shapes which will independently fill a surface without leaving any gap. Each of these shapes has its rules and organizational behaviour for achieving unity in space. For example, the triangle itself is threefold symmetry. Symmetry is the controlling factor of the Islamic pattern and is the reflection of unity. **The circle is the principle of all geometric pattern. Therefore, it too is a symbol of unity. Its inner aspect is the hidden centre becoming the dimensionless point of the compassing space.**

The equality of the paths from the origin symbolizes eternity; this is because the circle is without beginning or end. '*Ahad*' means equality; equality means symmetry. Threefold symmetry is the three equal paths which make up the triangle which symbolizes consciousness and the minimal biological needs: digestion, absorption and excretion. The important factor is the triangular relationship between sun, earth and moon. Three giving rise to six, is very significant in Islam. The spiritual triangle is important since it appears at the beginning of each sura of the Quran.

'*Allah, Rahman and Rahin.*'

'A L M This is the book in its guidance sure, without doubt, to those who fear God.'

The square is a product of four equal paths which represent unity. It symbolizes the earth. The triangle or human consciousness and the hexagon or circle represent heaven.

God created the human body with its multiplicity of cells. The cell is the part and the body is the whole. The health concept is based on the principles of the cell and the whole. In the same way the human body (the whole) as a person is individual, he is part of the whole world and the concept of the whole is based on geometrical principles *(Alim Al Mithal).* **Geometry is the link in the architecture of Islam. It is the principle behind the planning of cities, of buildings within the city and the windows, walls, grills and screens within these buildings.**

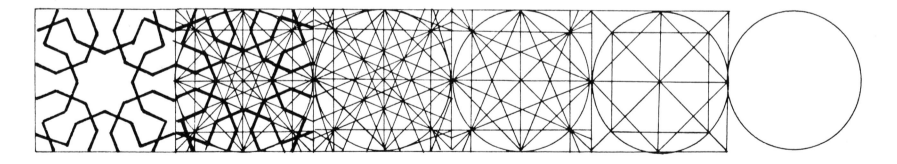

Islamic pattern

Meaning

'*Ala'l-baghi tadūrū da'iratū's Sawa'i.*'
(The transgressor shall eventually have his punishment.)

Hadith Sharif

'*The Baker*

'*Never will I forget a baker I passed by, rolling out his pastry in the twinkling of an eye.*

'*From when I saw it a ball in his hand to when it was spread out round as the moon, passed no more time than a circle takes to spread on the surface of a pool, when you throw a stone.*'

IBN AR-RUMI

According to the principle of geometry (*Alim Al Mithal*) the circle has significant meaning, representing equality, continuity and prosperity and it has always been a symbol of time. In Islam it represents the symbol of '*the first and the last*'. Houses of the Islamic world are usually covered with various decorations. **The predominant motif is the ornamental circle which is used to symbolize goodness and prosperity resulting from the vital life-giving rains which fall on the desert.**

Pilgrims Performing the Saay around the Kaaba

Planning

'*It would be a good thing if cities could develop an artistic pride leading them to mutual rivalry.*'

Bertrand Russell

'*Ma Kala ma Kafa Khain min ma latnir wa alha.*'
(That which is little in gravity, is better than that which is plenty but wastes time.)

The Right:

The principle of planning the urban structure of Arab cities should be based on the principle of unity, the 'Whole' being made up of cellular units containing positive and negative space, both having a covered or partially covered pedestrian and vehicular route.

The negative space is the open courtyard and the positive space is used functionally. The extension of the covered pedestrian and vehicular system will link these cellular units in such a way that the mirror reflection pattern will create other negative spaces. The scale of these spaces should not be vast and should indicate the enclosure of space. **The cellular unit should be made up of smaller segments** of equal form but each accommodating different functions.

Each segment should be flexible enough to change in size in order to achieve variety. Each segment contains a number of elements which can also be used in different ways to give variety to the shape of the segments.

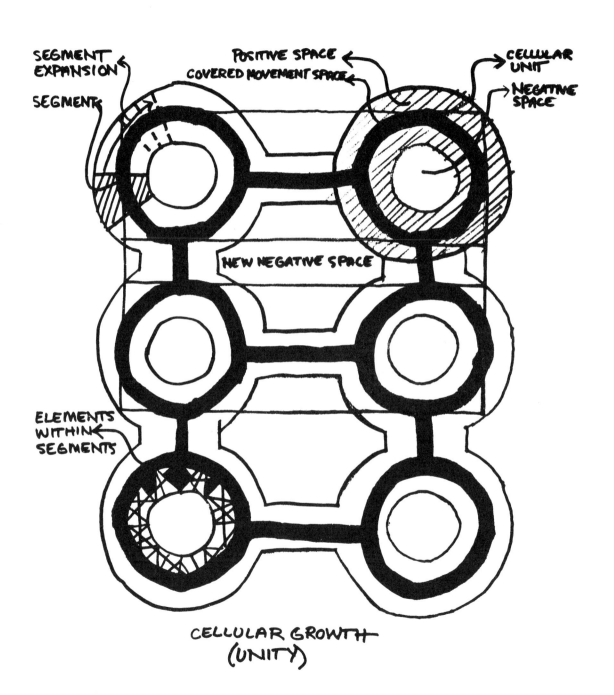

CELLULAR GROWTH
(UNITY)

The Wrong:

The wrong way of planning an Arab city is to rely on the concept of a 'detached machine for living'. Using this rigid approach to planning relies on the concept of the isolated tower block on a grid system. This is where spaces in-between are designed only for traffic and the buildings, designed as perfect functional units, are cut off from all public facilities. This concept is arrived at by devoting oneself entirely to the individual structure and its specific function and looking at each building as a free-standing monument.

The idea of the anatomy of the city being broken down into its functional components, the theory of compartmentalization of functions is very negative. In this case, the relationship between the various elements is only fragmentary and does not add up to an integrated system. **Here the design of the structures neglects the problem of urban space, it is very abstract and resembles a piece of graphic art.** If the shapes of the isolated units are changed to squares, crosses or even Y-shapes, this only illustrates how superficially the designer has coped with the urban space.

The isolated, functional-unit system is a disaster to the life of the community; city centres which contain nothing but shops and offices are deserted outside working hours and isolated residential complexes turn into dormitories. We should look towards an integration of the urban functions. The fascination of the project should be derived from a special composition with geometrically definable space expressed in pathways, courtyards and intermediate spaces. It would not be derived from a building as an isolated unit in its aesthetic completeness. The concepts of right and wrong planning are very sensitive to Islam. It is like the concept of *'Al Rahma wal igab'* (Mercy and Punishment).

'Ina Allah ghafour rahim wa ina adhabihi huwa al-adham al-alim.'
(God is forgiving and merciful and He is severe in His punishment.)

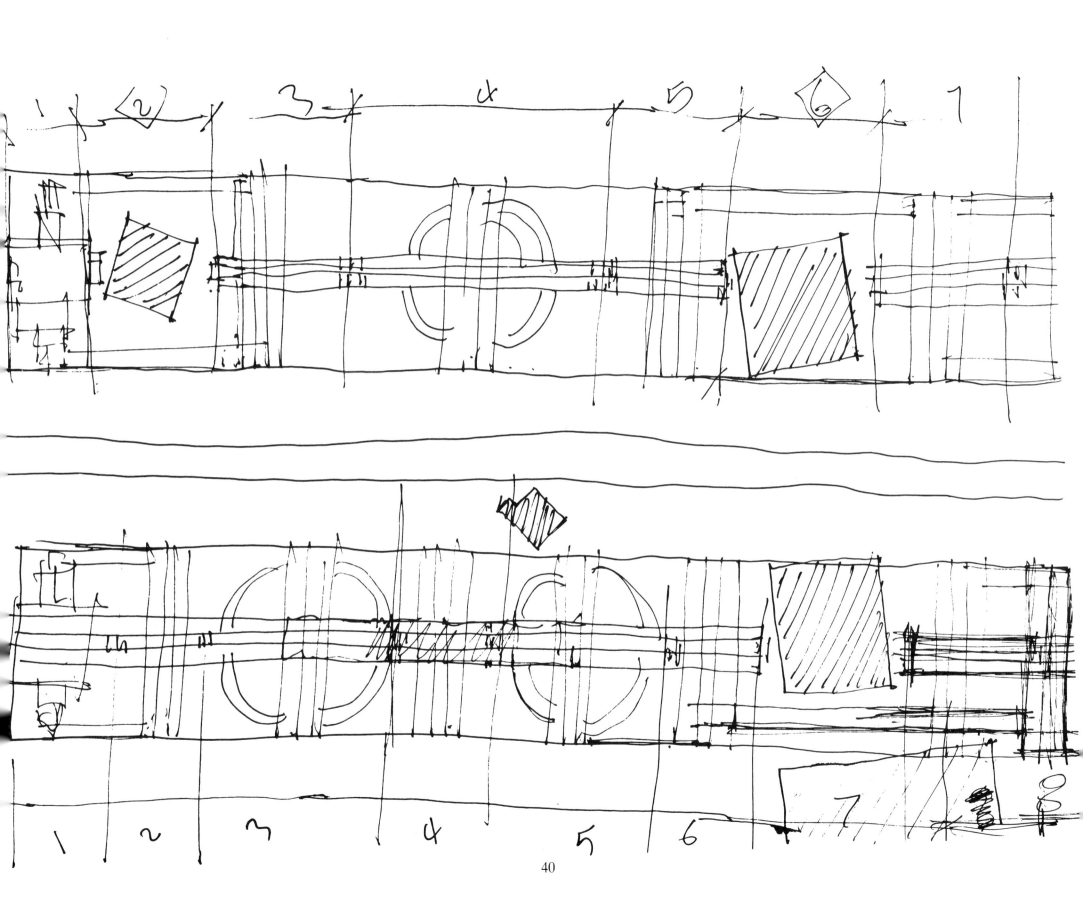

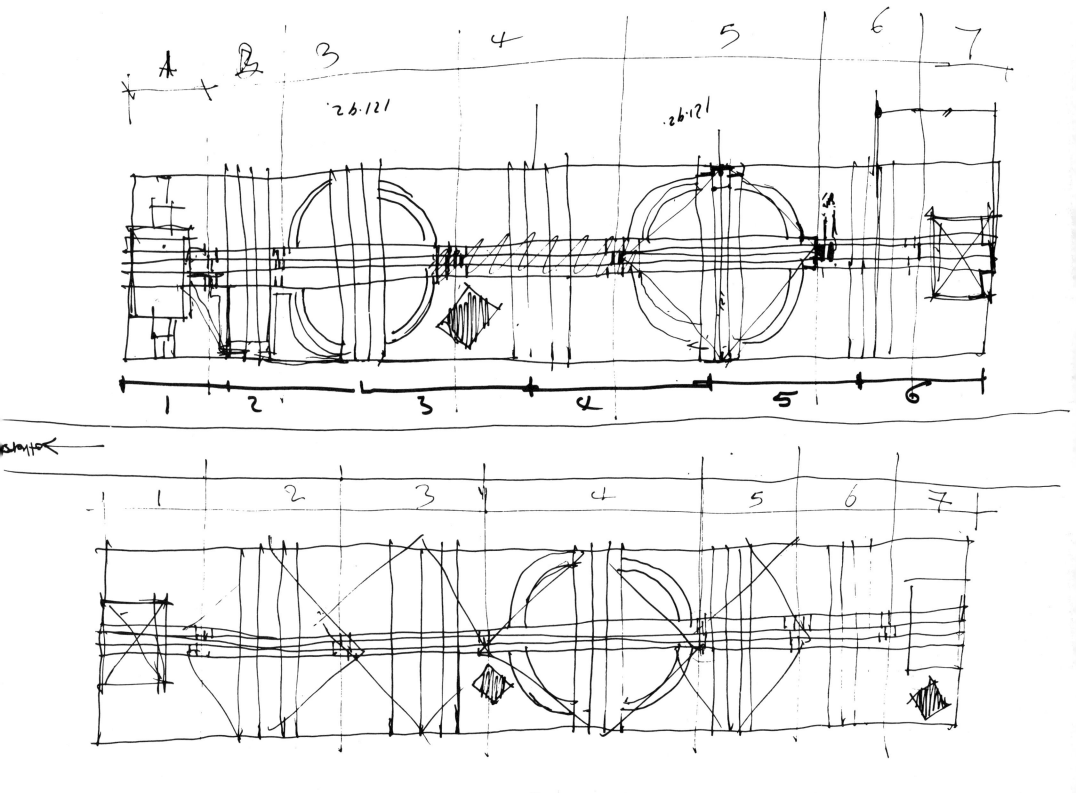

41

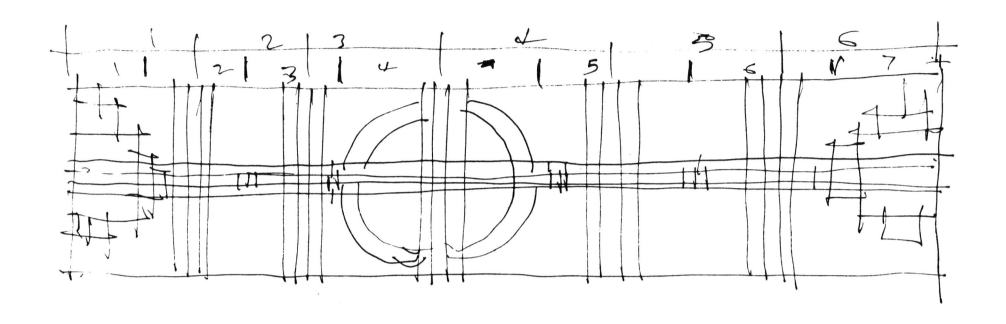

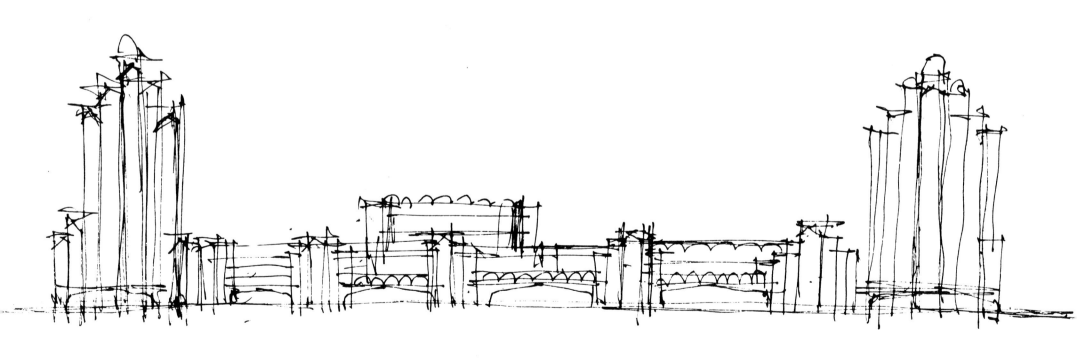

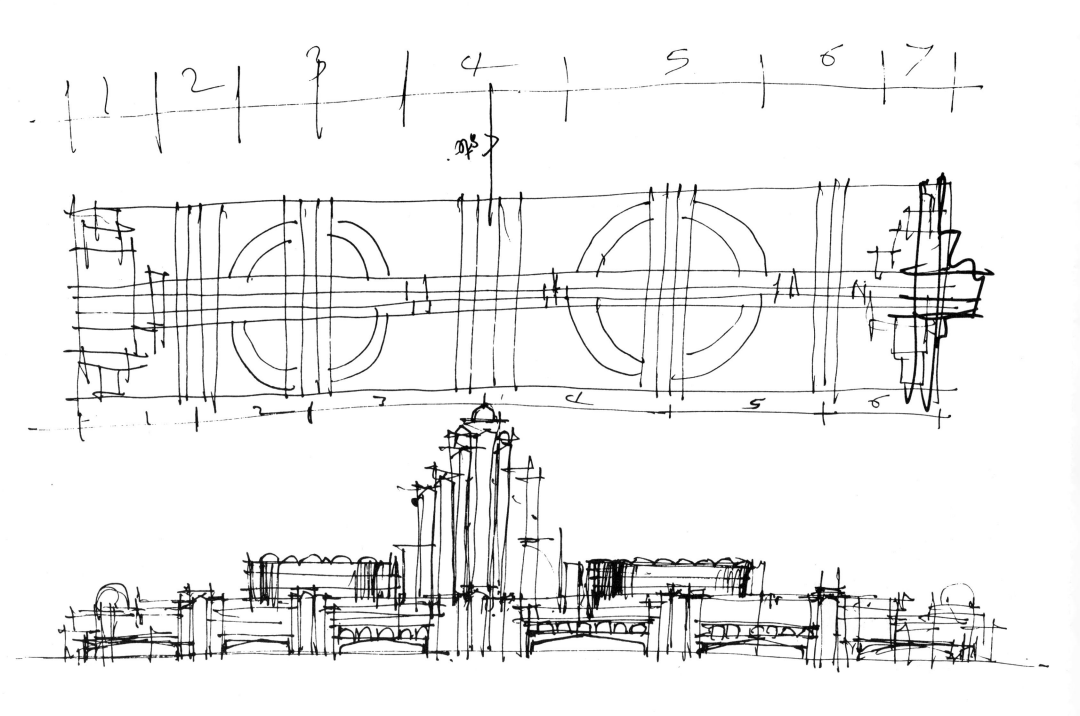

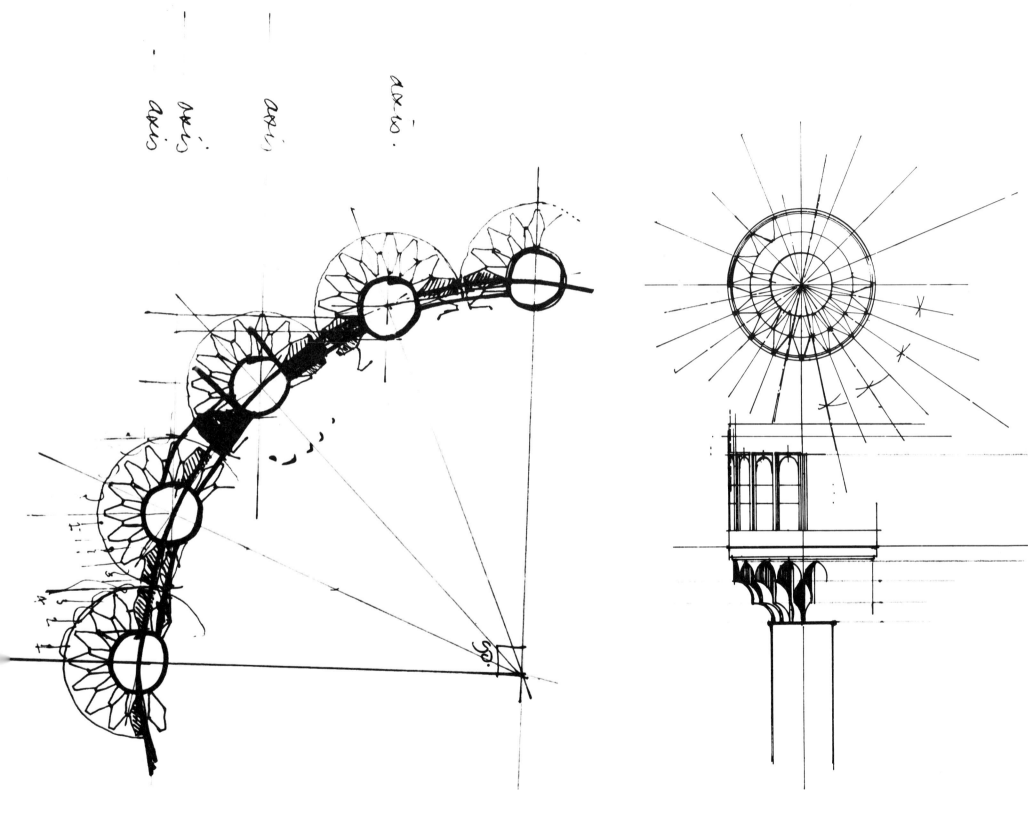

axis.
axis.
axis.
axis.
axis.

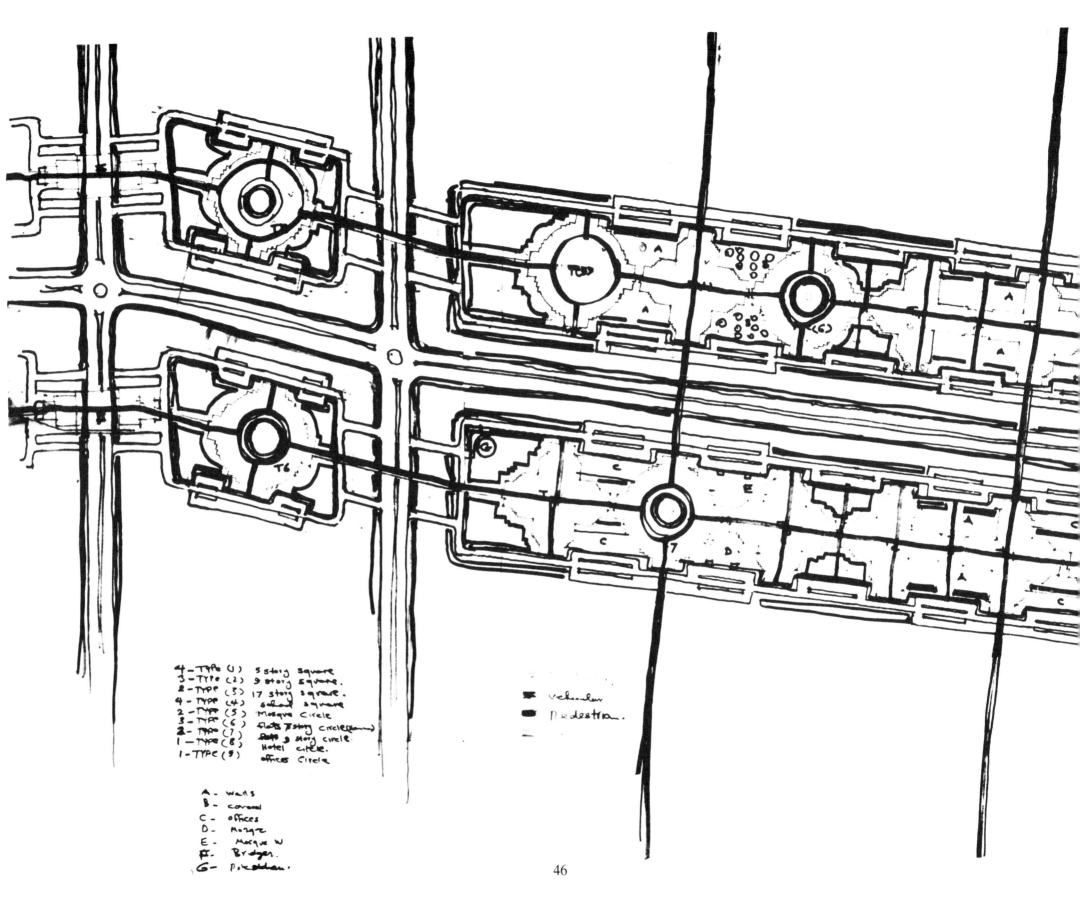

4 – Type (1)   5 story square
3 – Type (2)   9 story square.
8 – Type (3)   17 story square.
4 – Type (4)   school square
2 – Type (5)   Mosque Circle
3 – Type (6)   flats 8 story circle(garden)
2 – Type (7)   flats 9 story circle.
1 – Type (8)   Hotel circle.
1 – Type (9)   offices Circle

A – walls
B – canal
C – offices
D – Mosque
E – Mosque N
F – Bridges.
G – Pedestrian.

■ Vehicular
● Pedestrian.

46

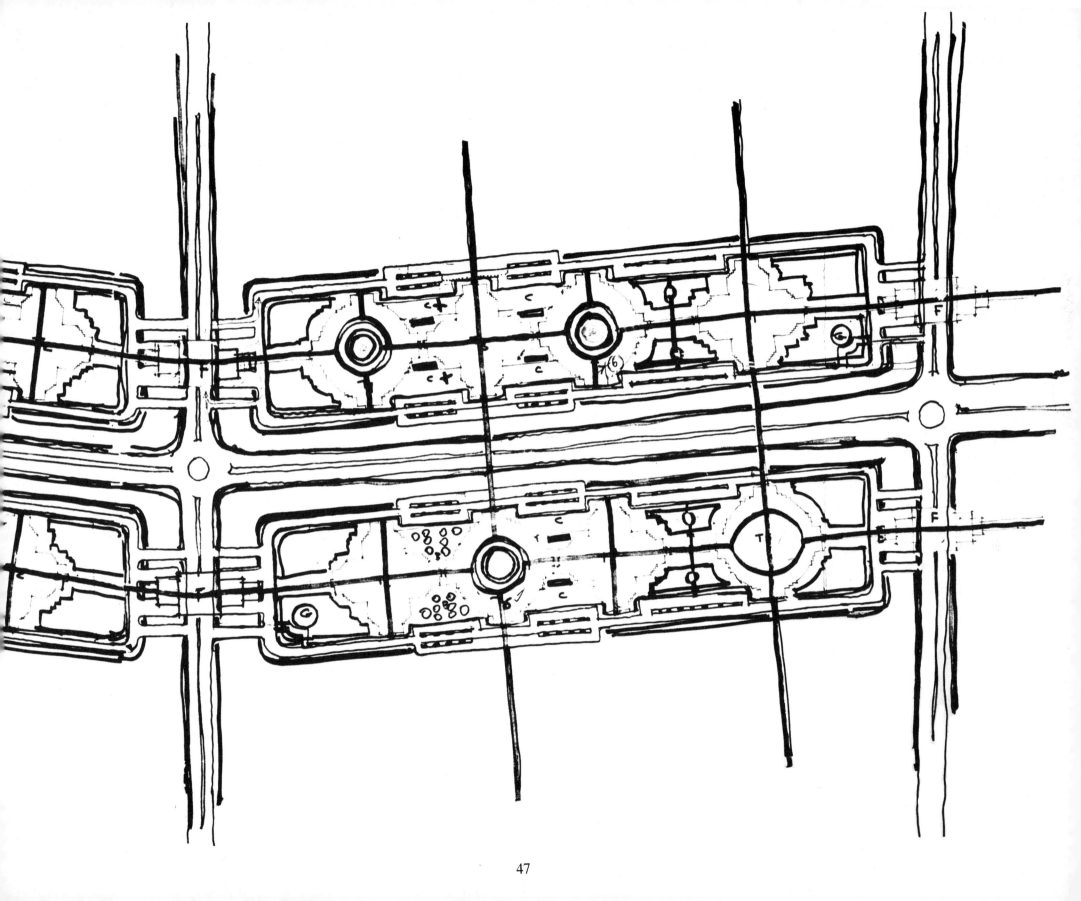

47

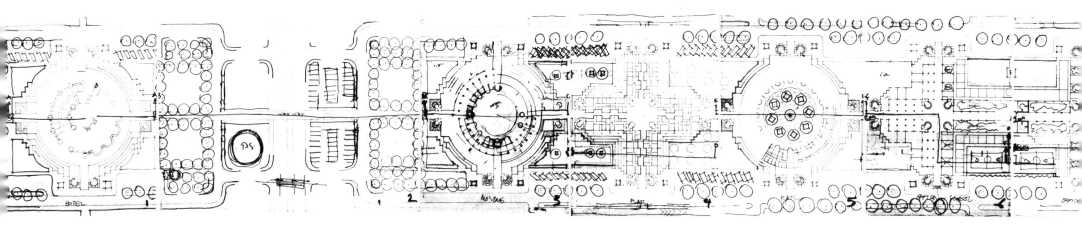

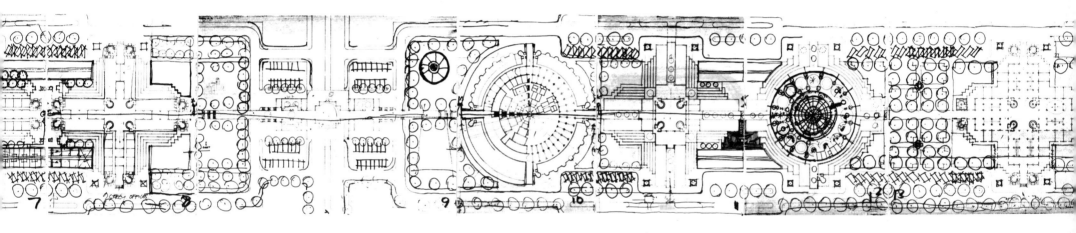

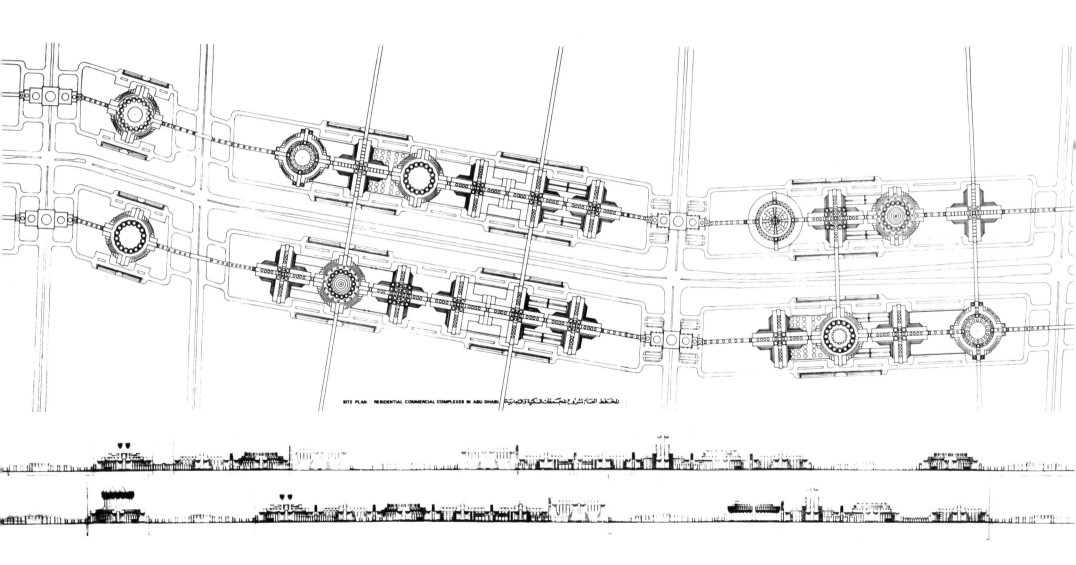

SITE PLAN. RESIDENTIAL COMMERCIAL COMPLEXES IN ABU DHABL المخطط العام : مشروع للمجمعات السكنية والتجارية

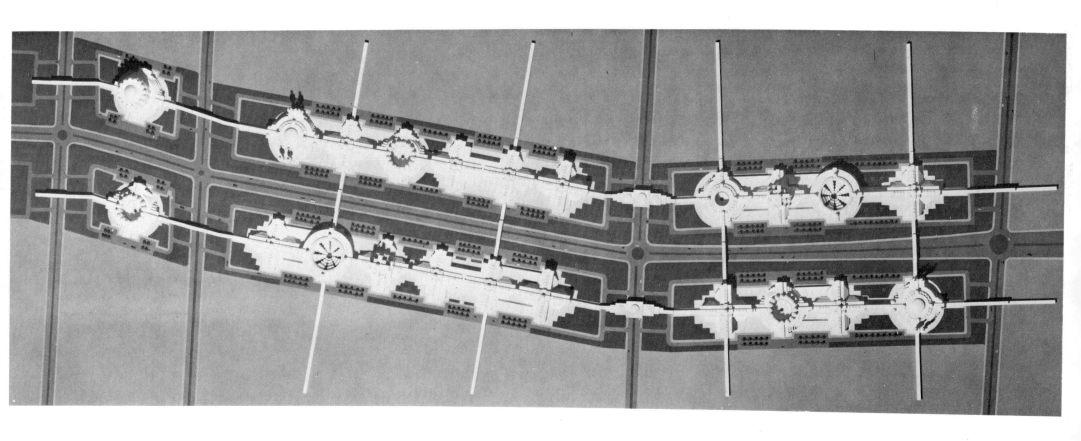

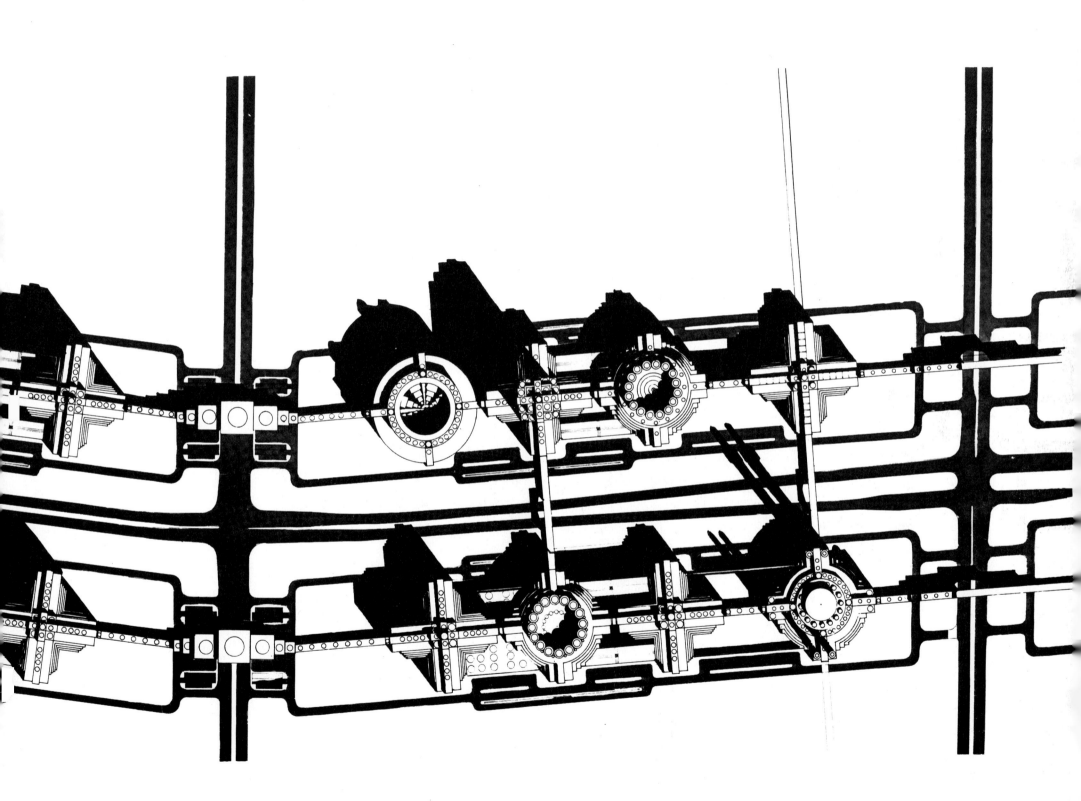

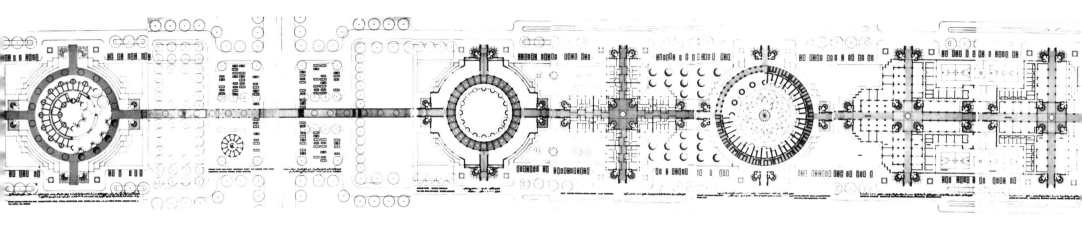

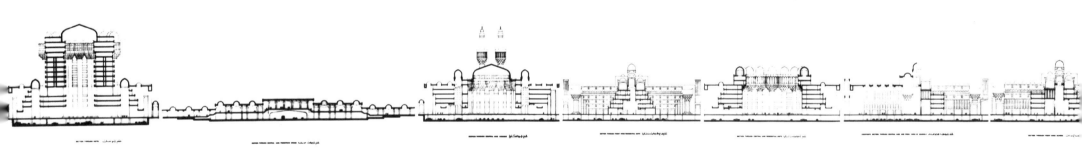

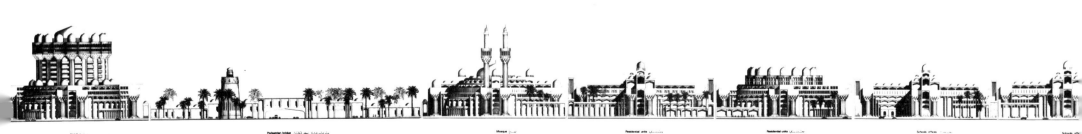

Hotel   Pedestrian bridge   Mosque   Residential units   Residential units   Schools offices   Schools offices

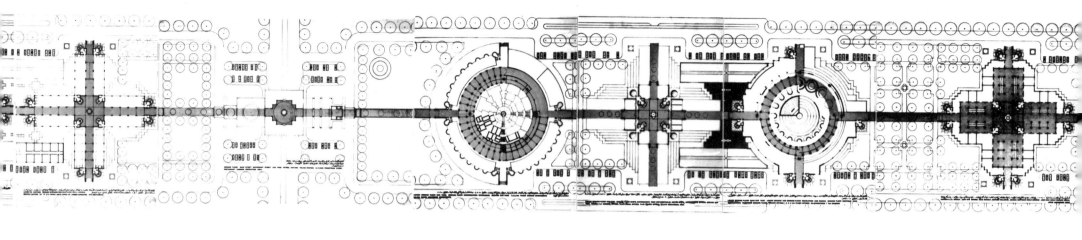

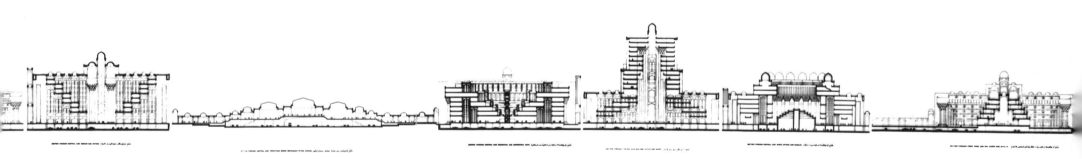

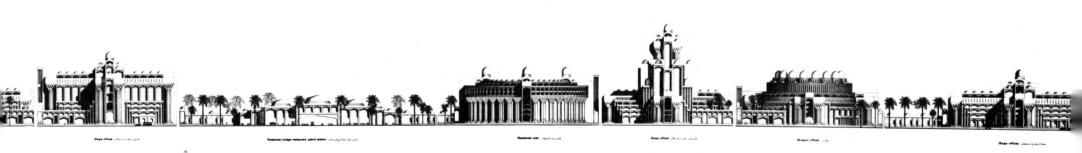

Shops-offices   Pedestrian bridge-restaurant-patrol station   Residential units   Shops-offices   Museum-offices   Shops-offices

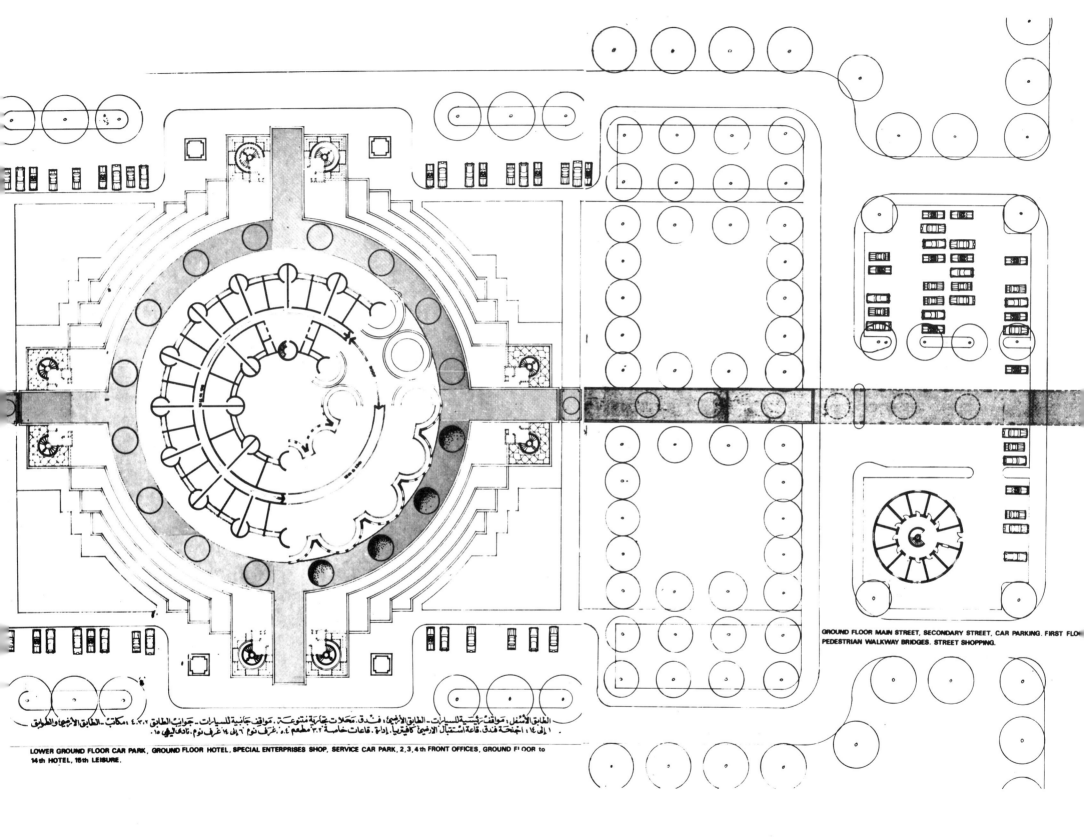

GROUND FLOOR MAIN STREET, SECONDARY STREET, CAR PARKING, FIRST FLO
PEDESTRIAN WALKWAY BRIDGES. STREET SHOPPING.

الطابق الأسفل مواقف رئيسية للسيارات ـ الطابق الأرضي فندق محلات تجارية متنوعة مواقف جانبية للسيارات ـ جوانب الطابق ٢،٣،٤ مكاتب ـ الطابق الأرضي والطوابق
١ إلى ١٤ أجنحة فندق، قاعة استقبال الأرضي كافيتريا، إدارة، قاعات خاصة ٣،٢ مطعم ٤، غرف نوم ٦ إلى ١٤ غرف نوم، نادي ليلي ١٥

LOWER GROUND FLOOR CAR PARK, GROUND FLOOR HOTEL, SPECIAL ENTERPRISES SHOP, SERVICE CAR PARK, 2,3,4th FRONT OFFICES, GROUND FLOOR to
14th HOTEL, 15th LEISURE.

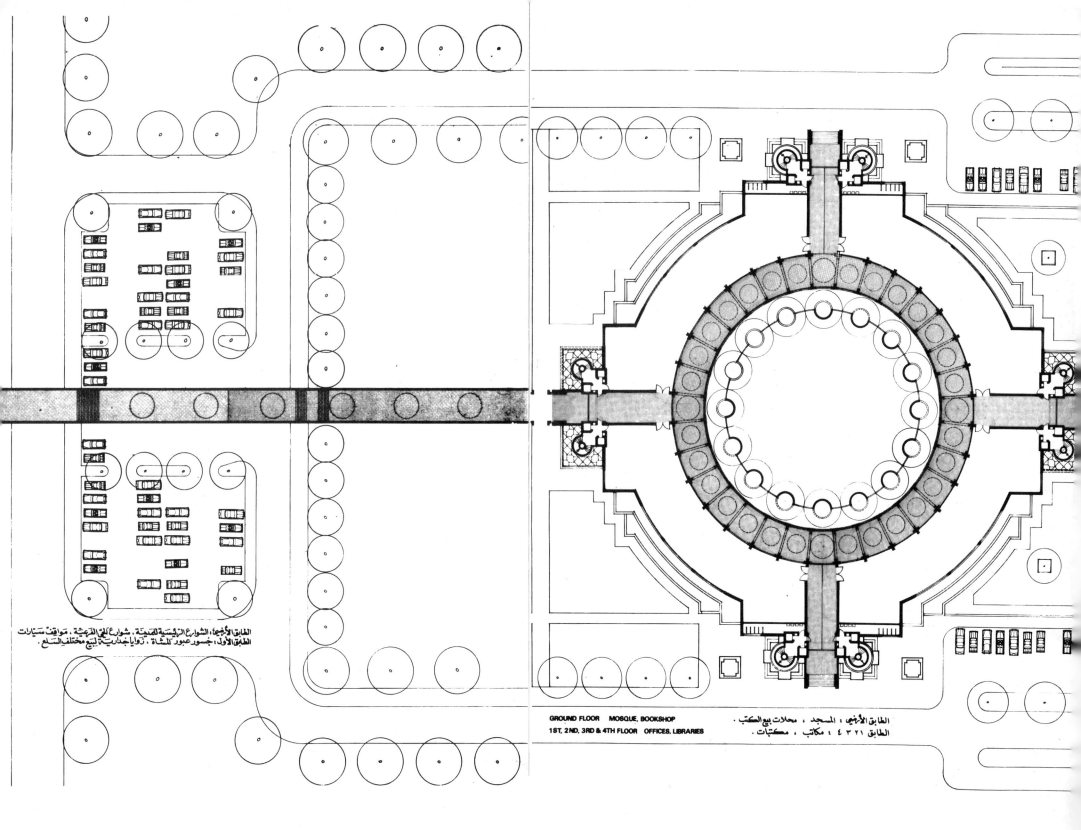

GROUND FLOOR   MOSQUE, BOOKSHOP
1ST, 2ND, 3RD & 4TH FLOOR   OFFICES, LIBRARIES

الطابق الأرضي : المسجد ، محلات بيع الكتب .

الطابق ١ ٢ ٣ ٤ : مكاتب ، مكتبات .

الطابق الأرضي، الشوارع الرئيسية للمدينة، شوارع الحي الفرعية ، مواقف سيارات
الطابق الأول : جسور عبور المشاة ، زوايا اخدارية لبيع مختلف السلع .

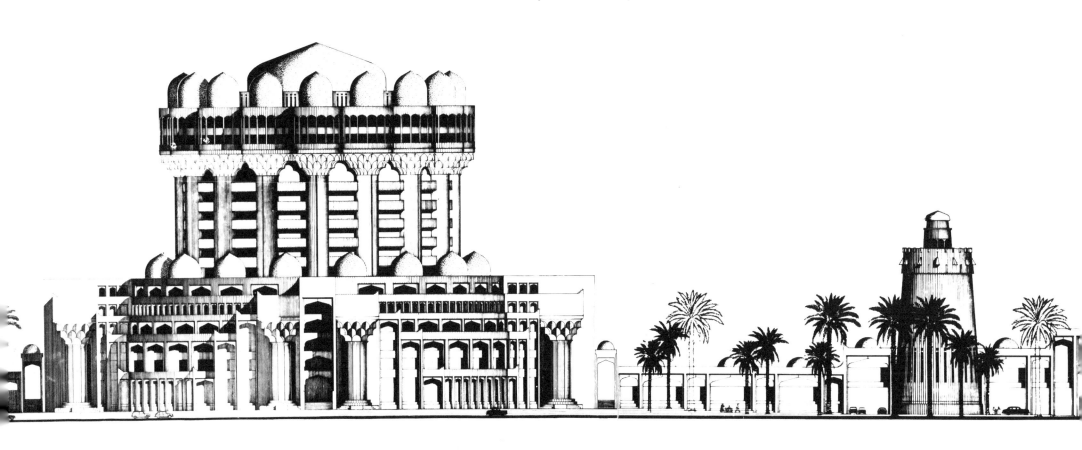

الفــــدق Hotel

58

estrian bridge جسر عبور المشاة . مركز شرطة.

Mosque الجامع

59

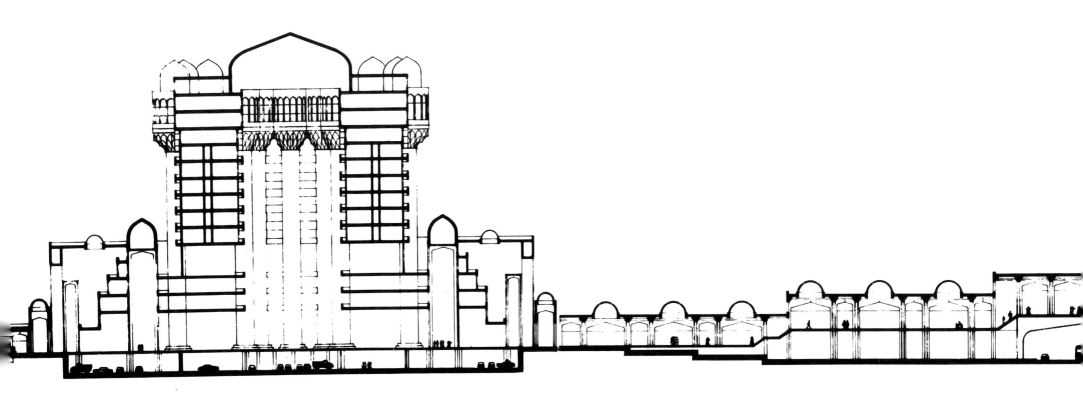

SECTION THROUGH HOTEL مقطع رأسى للفندق

SECTION THROUGH CENTRAL AXIS PE

60

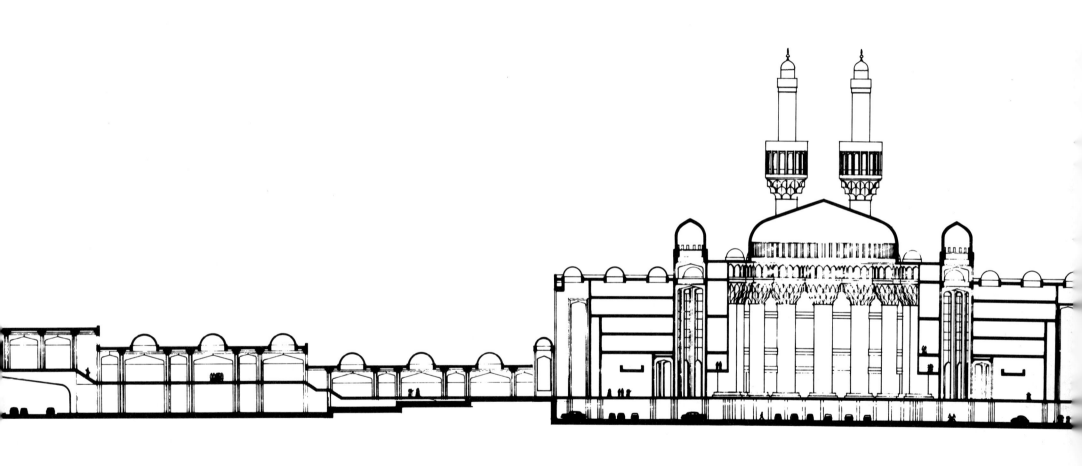

BRIDGE مقطع رئيسي للجسر عبور المشاة

61

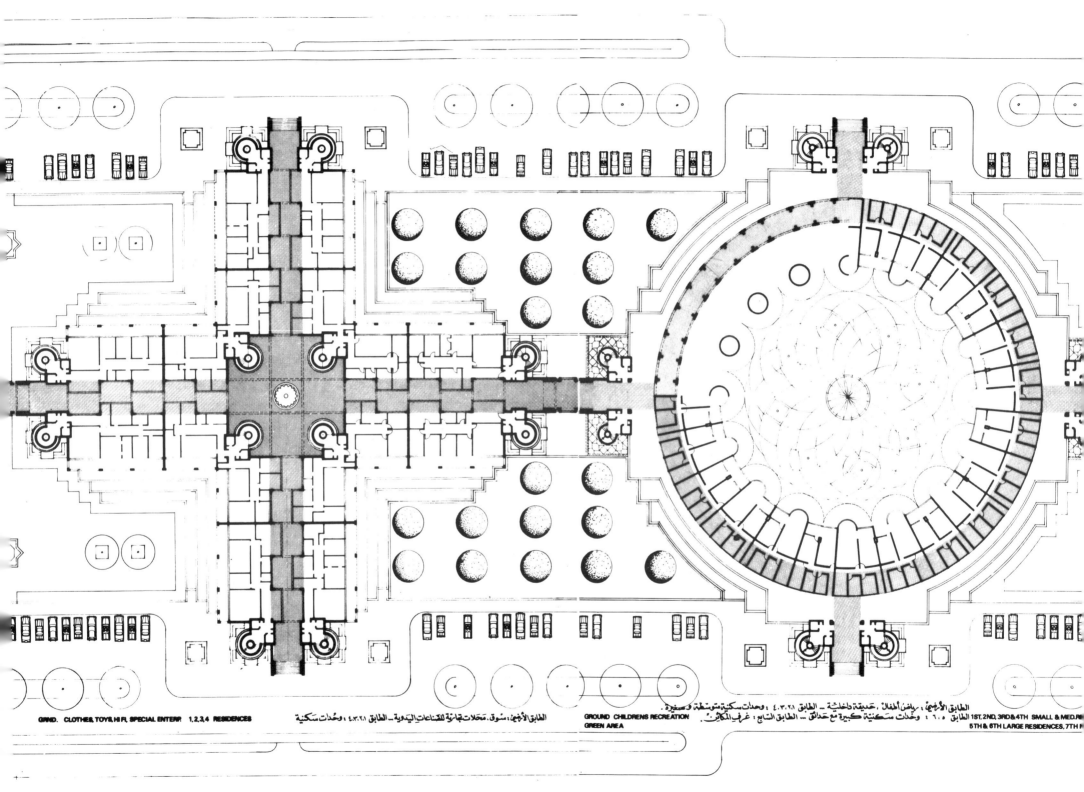

الطابق الأرضي : رياض الأطفال ، حديقة داخلية ـ الطابق ٤،٣،٢،١ وحدات سكنية متوسطة و صغيرة .

GRND. CLOTHES, TOYS, HI FI, SPECIAL ENTERP. 1,2,3,4 RESIDENCES

الطابق الأرضي : سوق ، محلات تجارية للصناعات اليدوية ـ الطابق ٤،٣،٢،١ وحدات سكنية

الطابق ٦،٥ : وحدات سكنية كبيرة مع حدائق ـ الطابق السابع : غرف المكاتب .

GROUND CHILDRENS RECREATION
GREEN AREA

5TH & 6TH LARGE RESIDENCES, 7TH F

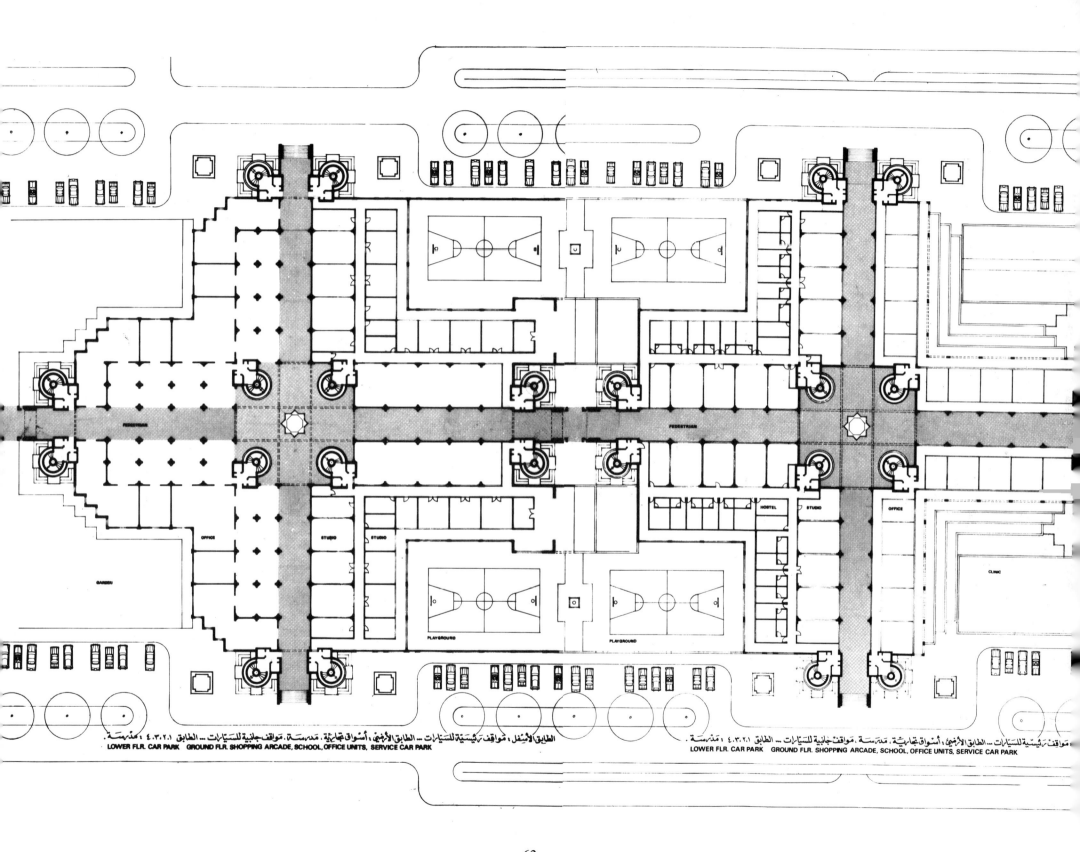

Residential units وحــدات سكنية   Residential units وحـــدات سكنية

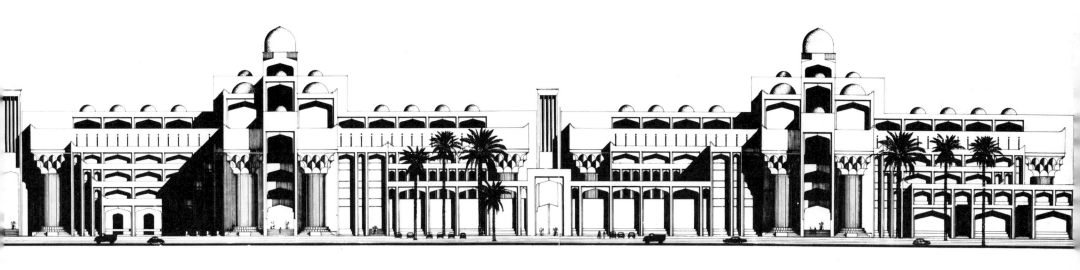

Schools-offices. مكاتب ومدارس

Schools-offices. المدارس والمكاتب

65

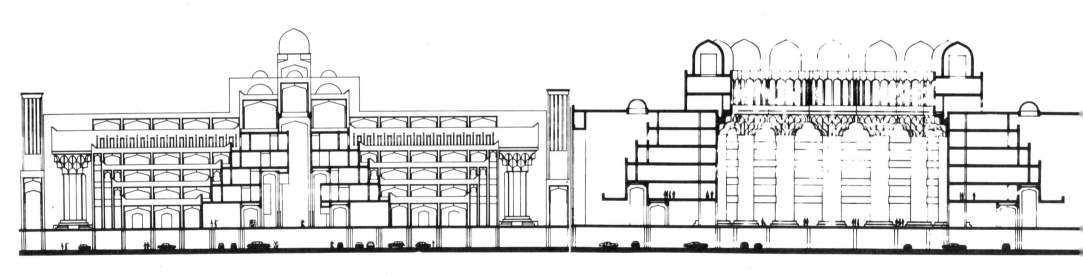

SECTION THROUGH FRONT WING RESIDENTIAL UNITS. مقطع الجناح الأمامي للوحدات السكنية.

SECTION THROUGH CENTRAL AXIS RESIDENTIAL UNITS. مقطع رئيسي للوحدات السكنية.

66

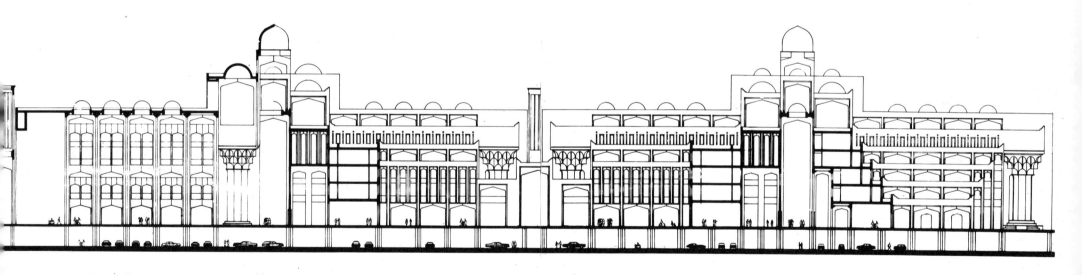

COMPOSITE SECTION THROUGH CENTRAL AXIS AND FRONT WING OF SCHOOLS . مقطع رئيسي والجناح الأمامي للمدارس

SECTION THROUGH FRONT WING SCHOOL مقطع رئيسي الجناح المدارس

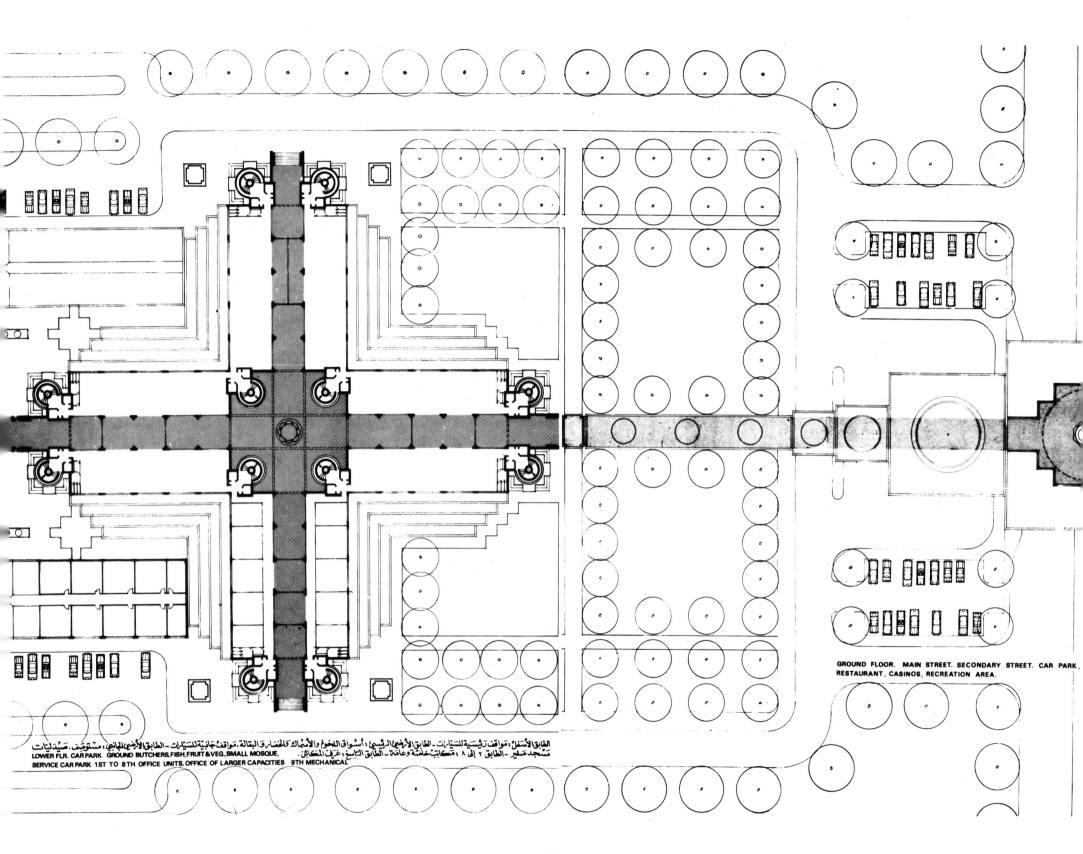

الطابق الأسفل : مواقف رئيسية للسيارات - الطابق الأرضي الرئيسي : أسواق اللحوم والأسماك والخضار والبقالة. مواقف جانبية للسيارات - الطابق الأرضي المباني : مستوصف . صيدليات .
مسجد صغير - الطابق ٢ إلى ٨ : مكاتب خاصة وعامة - الطابق التاسع : غرف المكائن .

LOWER FLR. CAR PARK   GROUND BUTCHERS, FISH, FRUIT & VEG, SMALL MOSQUE,
SERVICE CAR PARK 1ST TO 8TH OFFICE UNITS, OFFICE OF LARGER CAPACITIES 9TH MECHANICAL

GROUND FLOOR. MAIN STREET. SECONDARY STREET. CAR PARK,
RESTAURANT, CASINOS, RECREATION AREA.

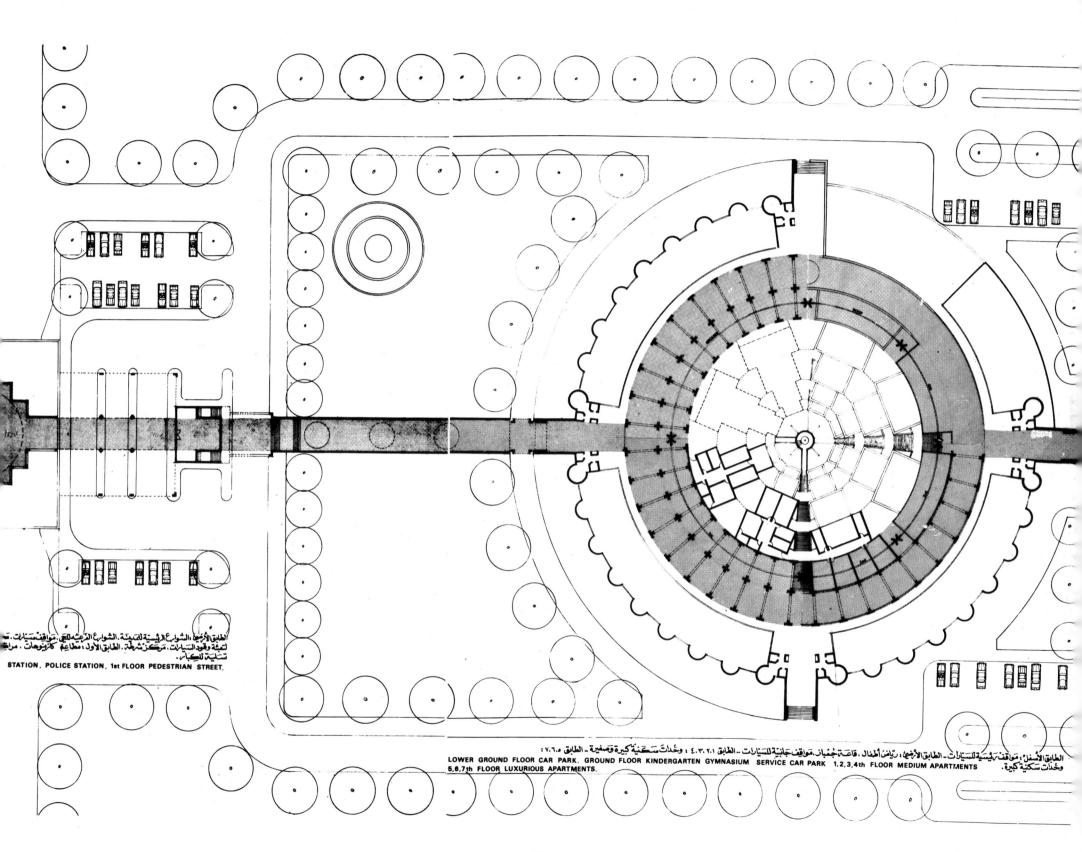

Shops-offices الاسواق التجارية والمكاتب

Pedestrian bridge-restaurant-petrol st

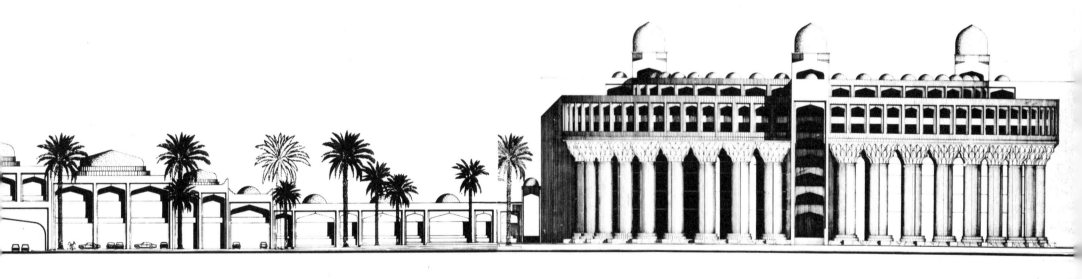

جسور عبور المشاة مع خدمات.

الوحــــدات السكنية. **Residential units**

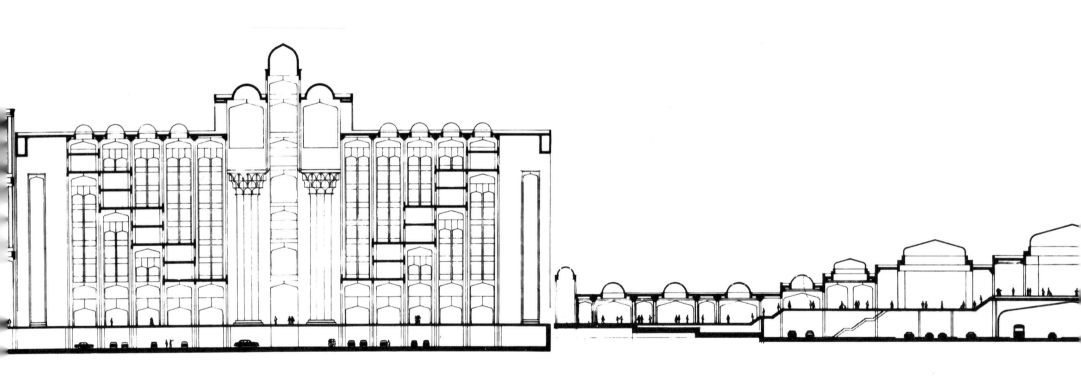

SECTION THROUGH CENTRAL AXIS MEDIUM SIZE OFFICES. مقطع رأسي في المكاتب المبني المتوسط الارتفاع

SECTION THROUGH CENTRAL AXIS PEDESTRIAN BRIDGE, RESTAURANT, PETROL.

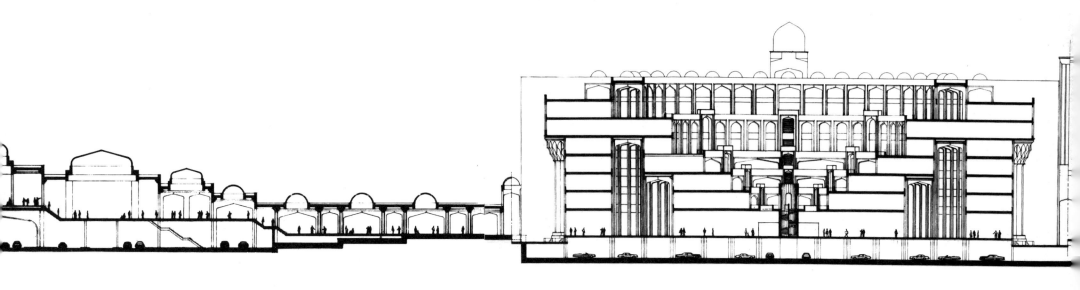

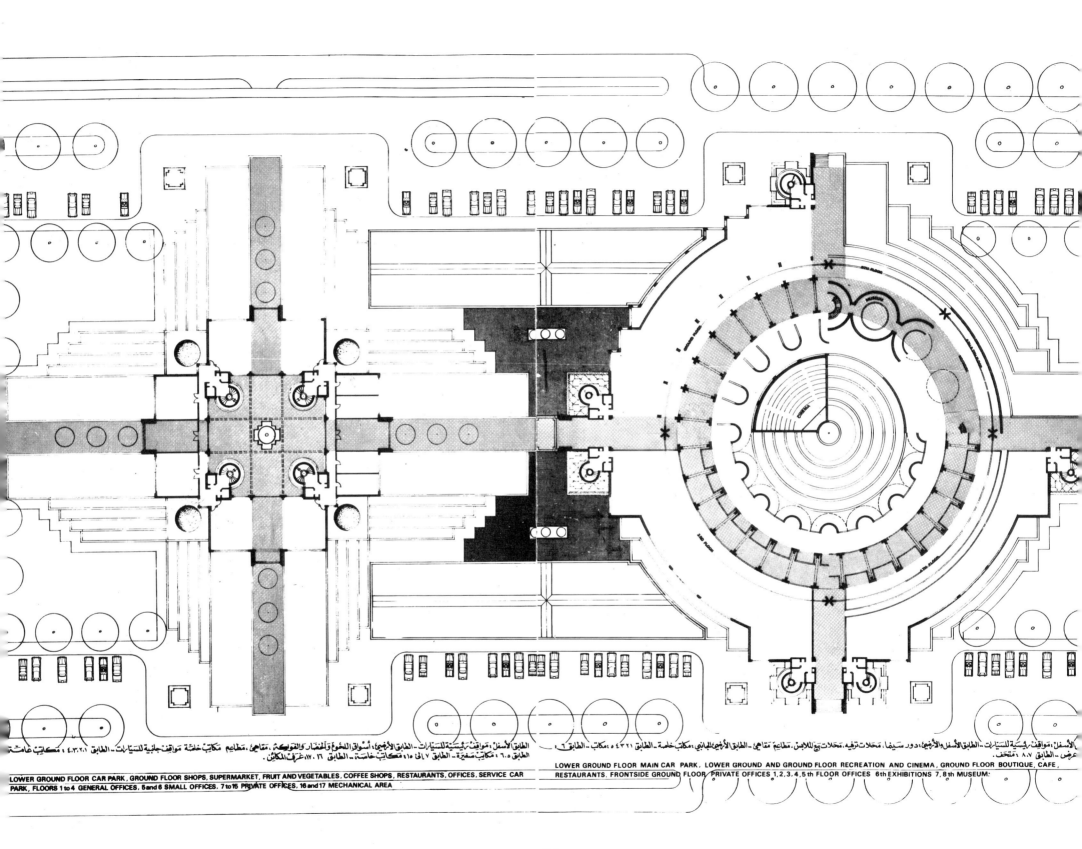

الطابق الأسفل : مواقف رئيسية للسيارات ، مواقف رئيسية للسيارات - الطابق الأرضي : دور سيفا ، محلات ترفيه ، محلات بيع الملابس ، مطاعم مقاهي - الطابق الأرضي الجانبي : مكاتب خاصة ١ ٢ ٣ ٤ ٥ - مكاتب - الطابق

الأسفل : مواقف رئيسية للسيارات ، مواقف رئيسية للسيارات - الطابق الأرضي : أسواق اللحوم والخضار والفواكة ، مقاهي ، مطاعم ، مكاتب خاصة - مواقف جانبية للسيارات - الطابق

LOWER GROUND FLOOR MAIN CAR PARK, LOWER GROUND AND GROUND FLOOR RECREATION AND CINEMA, GROUND FLOOR BOUTIQUE, CAFE,
RESTAURANTS. FRONTSIDE GROUND FLOOR PRIVATE OFFICES 1,2,3,4,5th FLOOR OFFICES 6th EXHIBITIONS 7,8 th MUSEUM.

LOWER GROUND FLOOR CAR PARK, GROUND FLOOR SHOPS, SUPERMARKET, FRUIT AND VEGETABLES, COFFEE SHOPS, RESTAURANTS, OFFICES, SERVICE CAR
PARK, FLOORS 1 to 4 GENERAL OFFICES, 5 and 6 SMALL OFFICES, 7 to 15 PRIVATE OFFICES, 16 and 17 MECHANICAL AREA

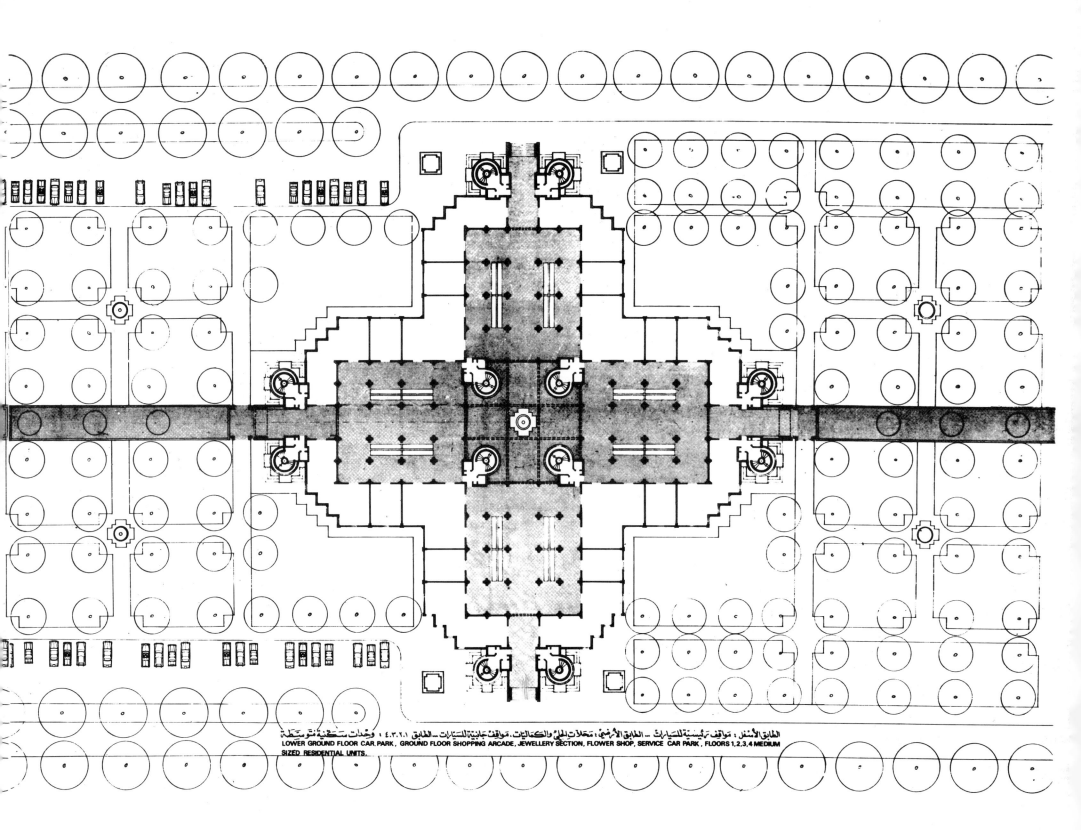

الطابق الأسفل : مواقف رئيسية للسيارات – الطابق الأرضي : محلات الحلي والكماليات، مواقف جانبية للسيارات – الطابق ١،٢،٣،٤ وحدات سكنية متوسطة

LOWER GROUND FLOOR CAR.PARK, GROUND FLOOR SHOPPING ARCADE, JEWELLERY SECTION, FLOWER SHOP, SERVICE CAR PARK, FLOORS 1,2,3,4 MEDIUM SIZED RESIDENTIAL UNITS.

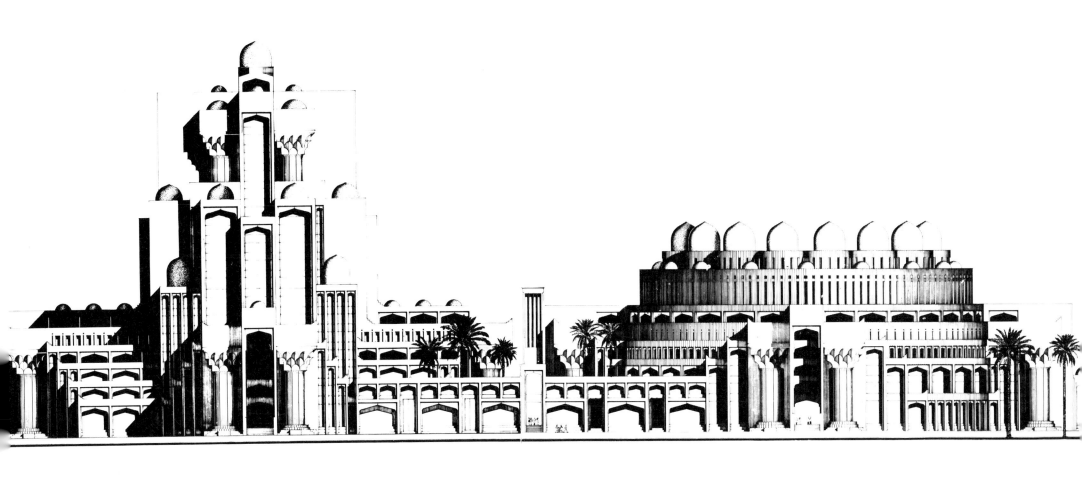

Shops-offices الأسواق التجارية والمكاتب   Museum-offices المكاتب

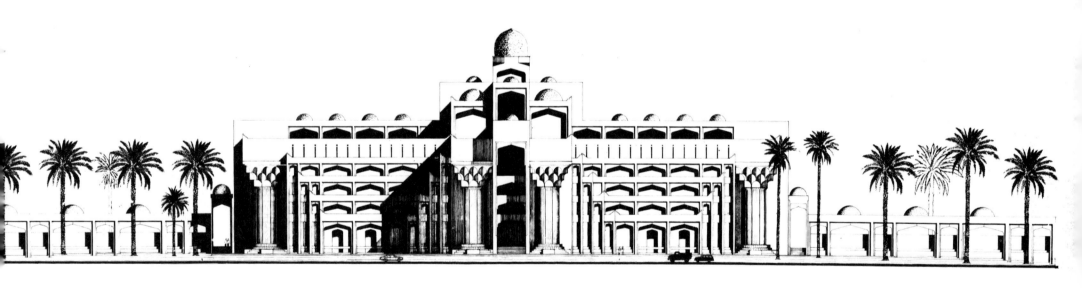

Shops-offices محلات تجارية ومكاتب

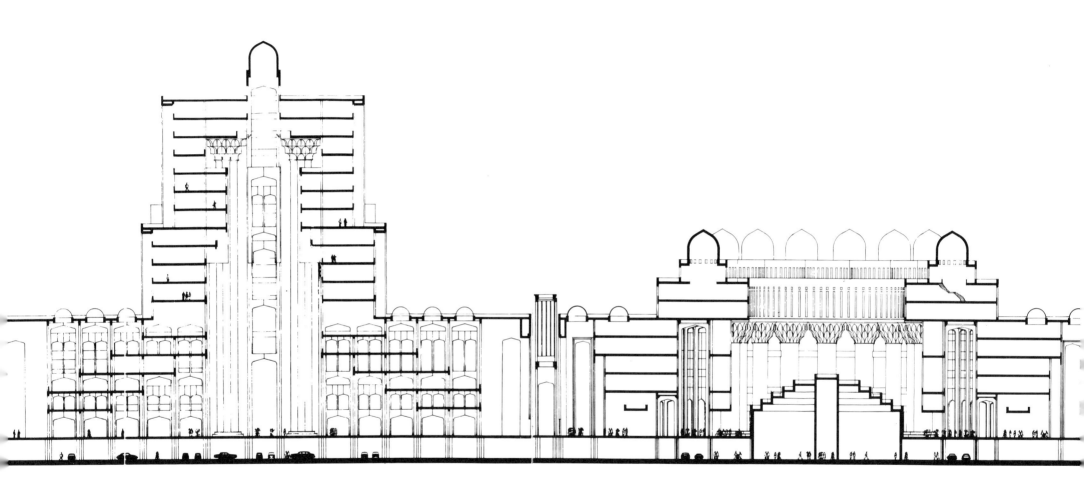

SECTION THROUGH CENTRAL AXIS SHOPS, OFFICES AND MUSEUM . مقطع رئيسى للمحلات التجارية والمكاتب .

SECTION THROUGH CENTRAL AXIS HIGH RISE OFFICES AND SHOPS . مقطع رئيسى للمكاتب المبنى العالى الارتفاع .

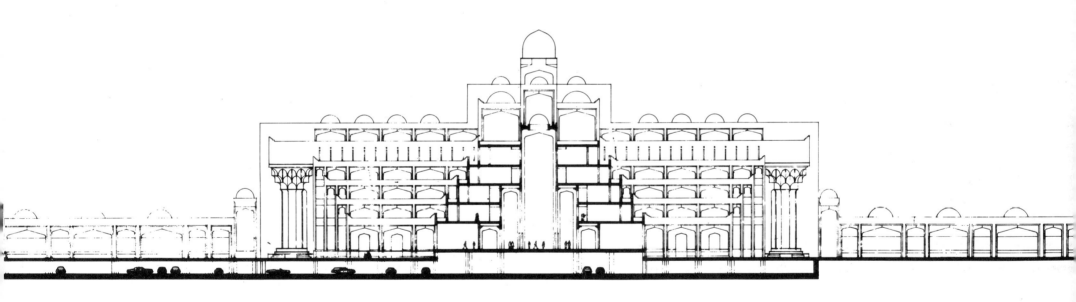

SECTION THROUGH FRONT WING LOW RISE SHOPS AND OFFICES . مقطع أمامي للمحلات التجارية والمكاتب في المبنى المنخفض الارتفاع .

Schools-offices .المدارسُ والمكاتب

Shops-offices الاسواق التجارية والمكاتب

81

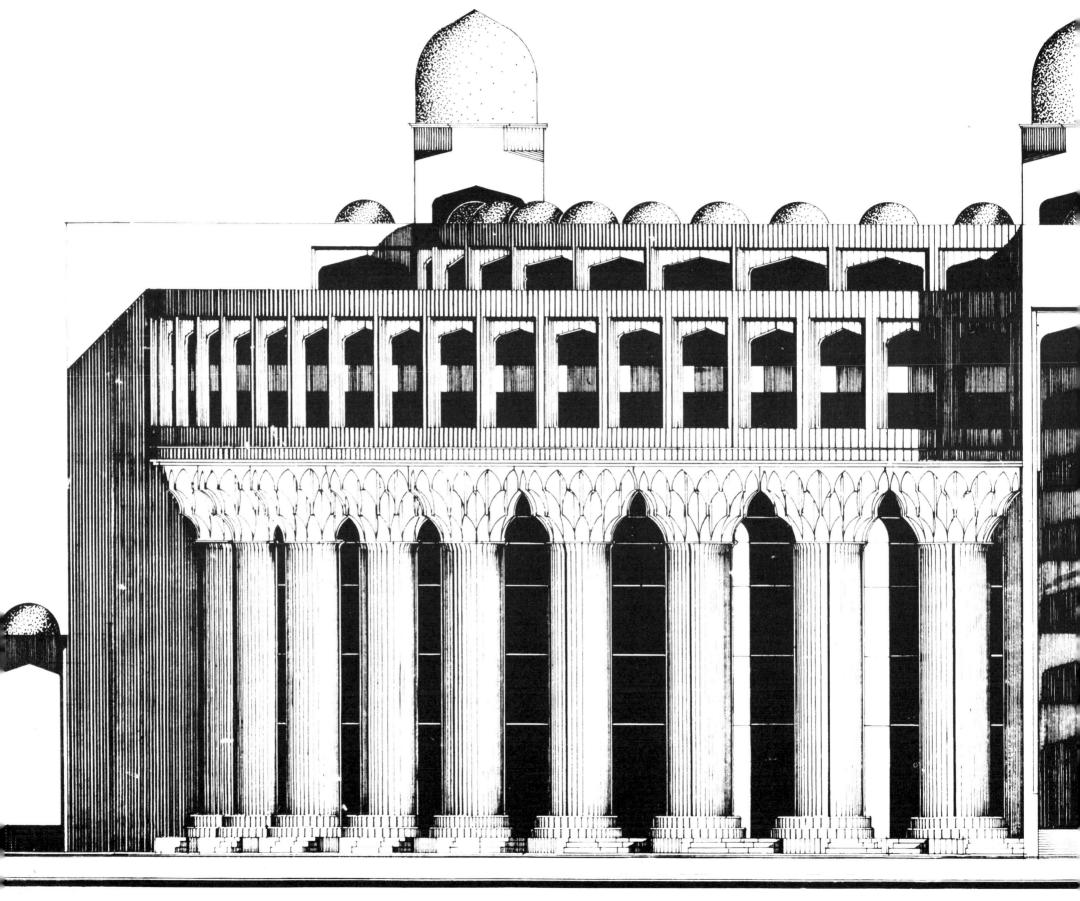

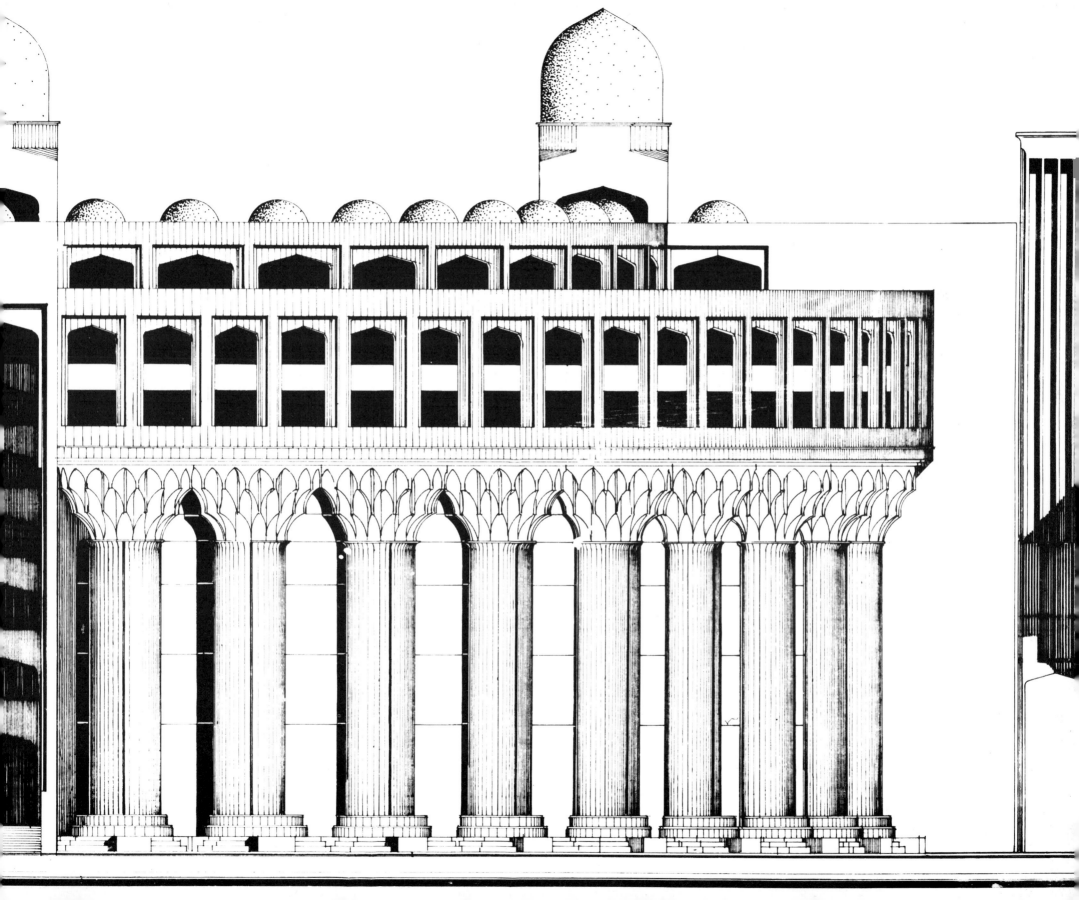

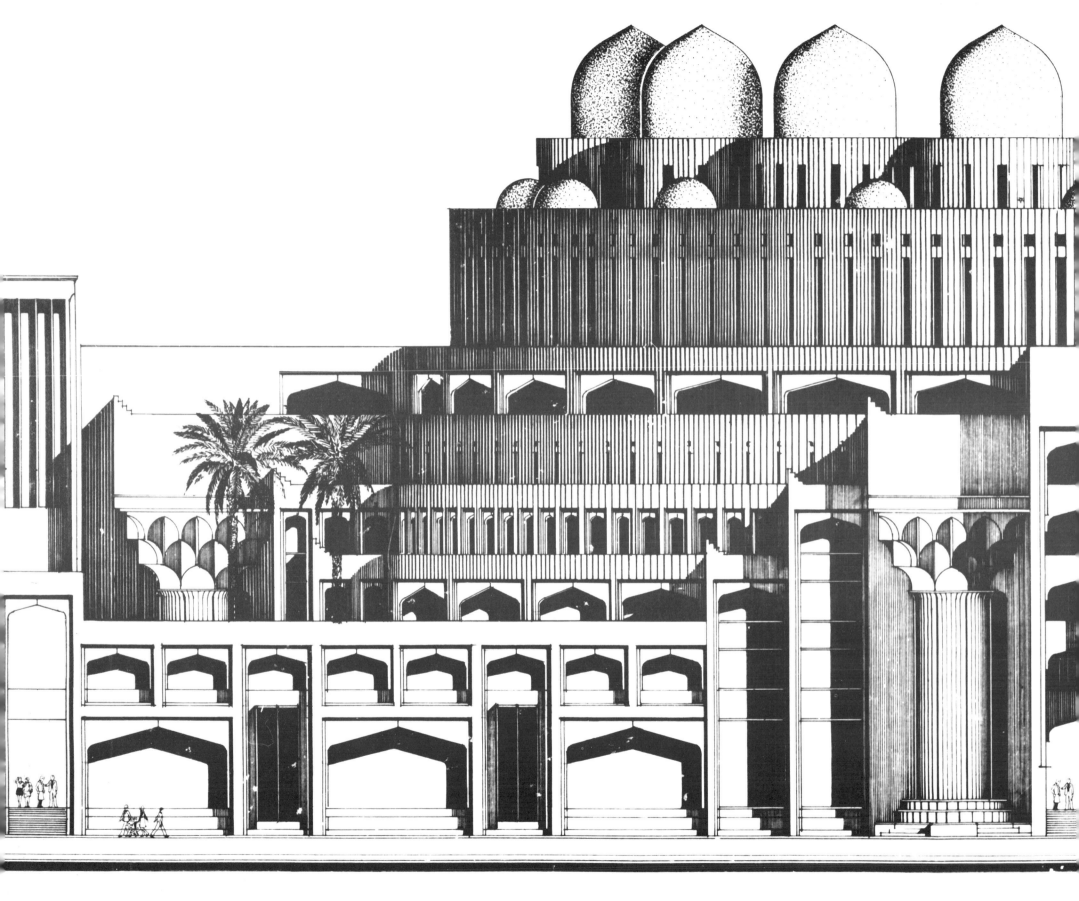

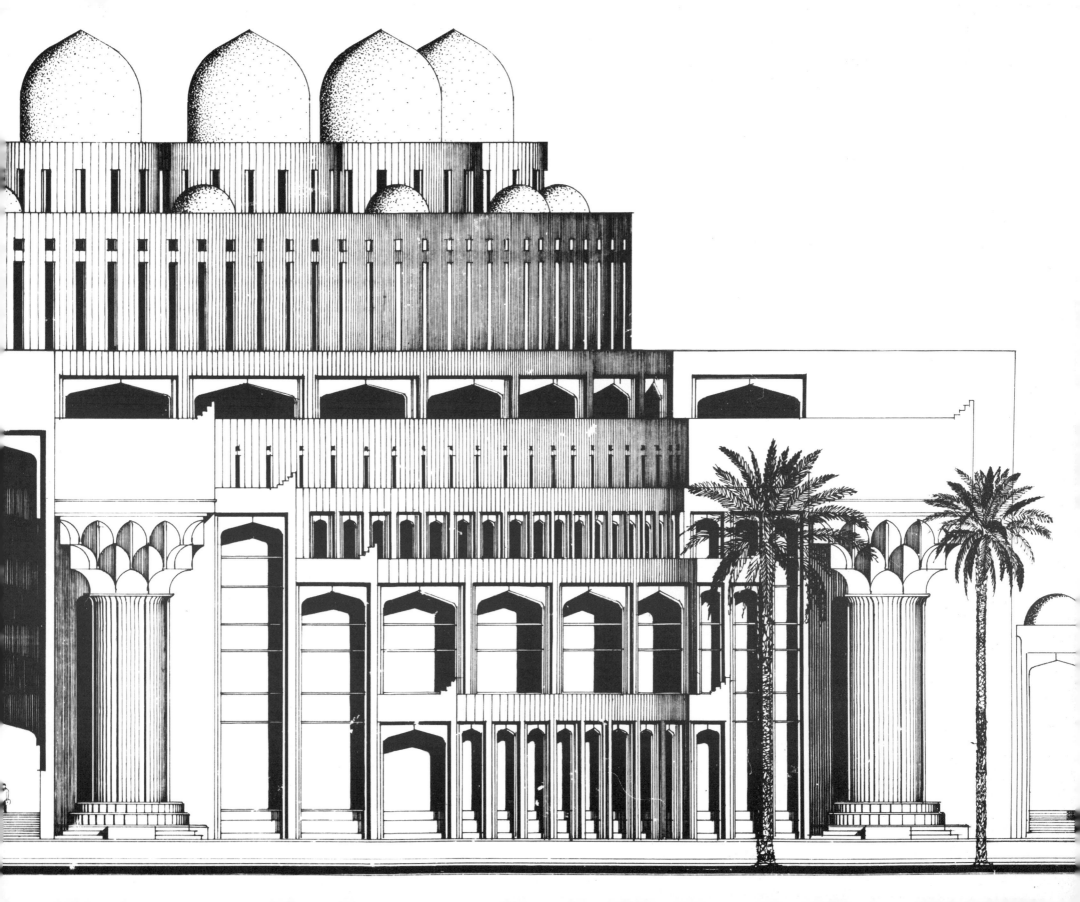

Shops-offices الأسواق التجارية والمكاتب

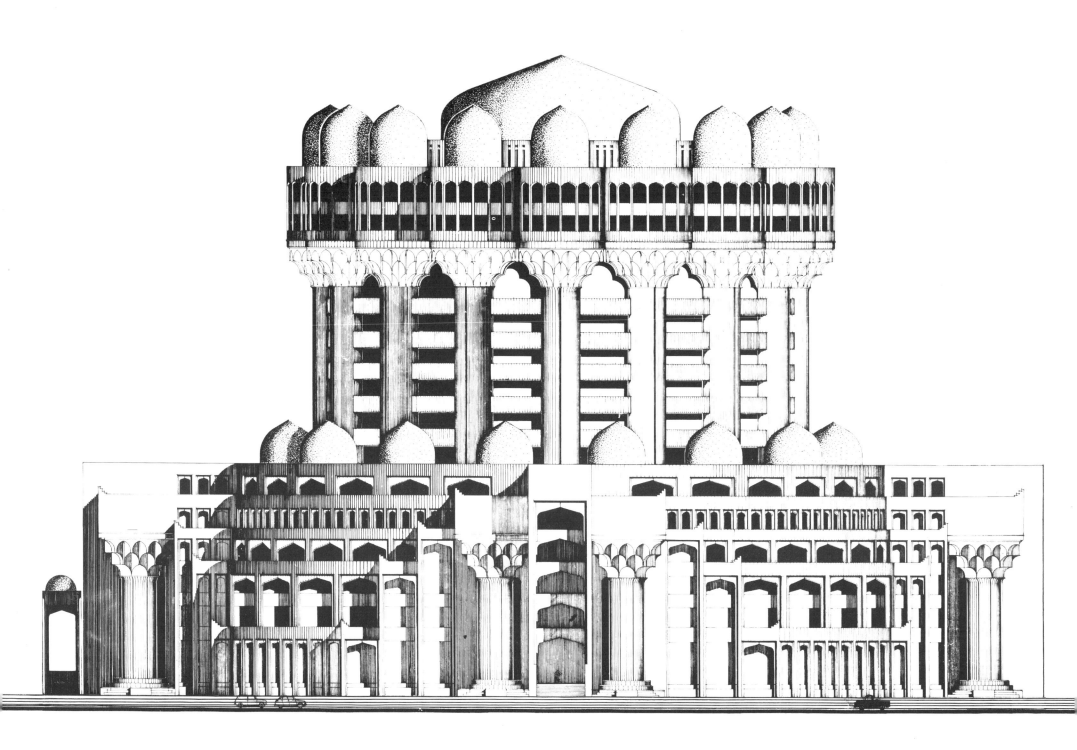

Hotel الفـنْـدق

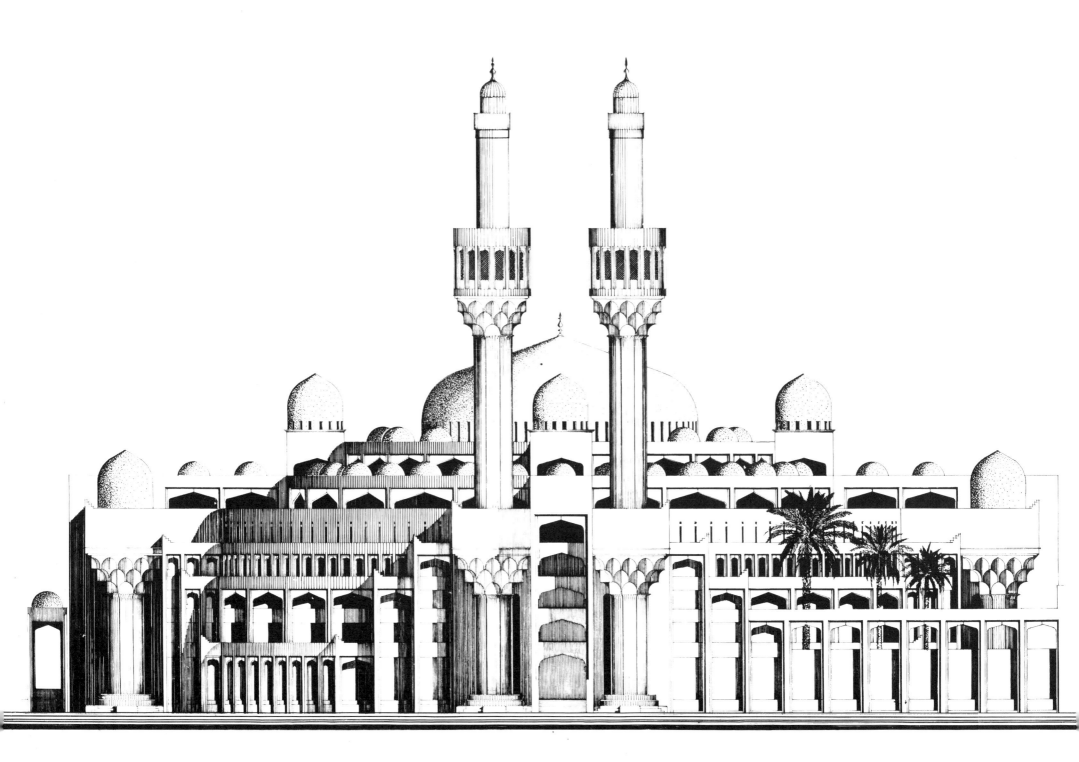

Mosque الجامع

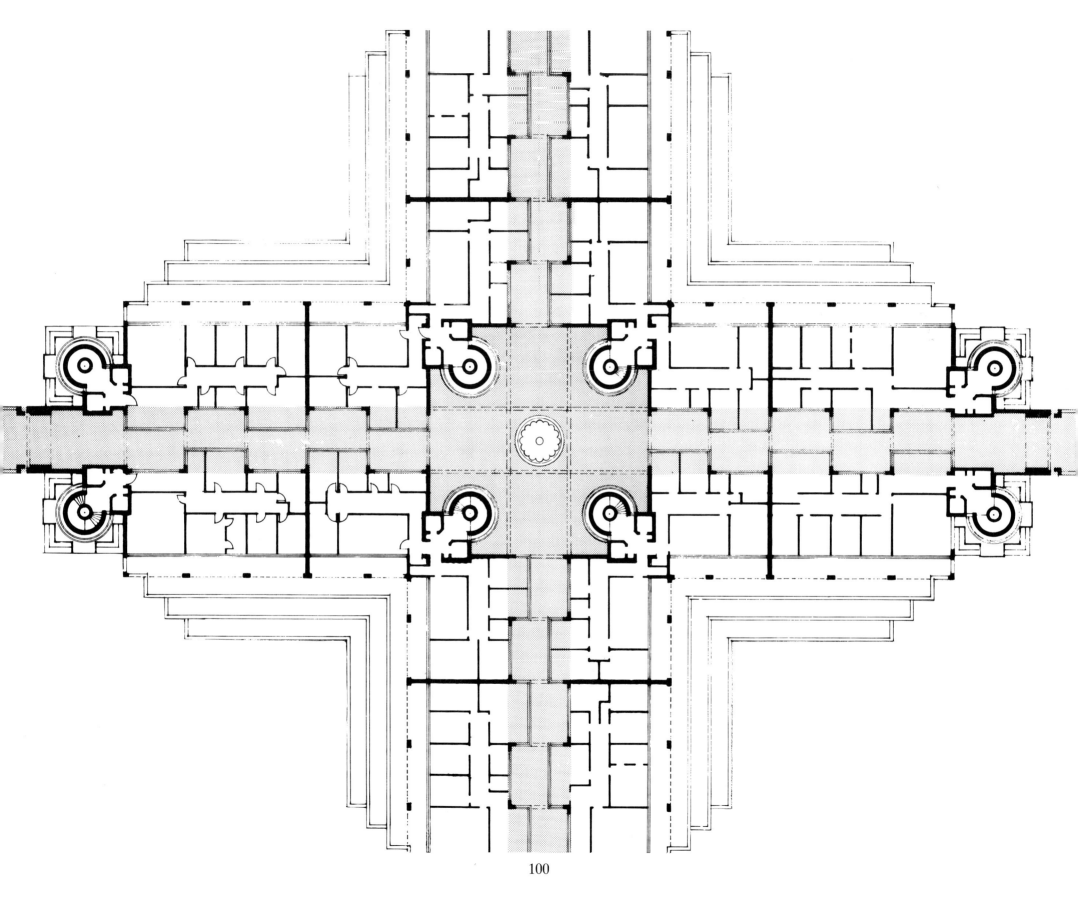

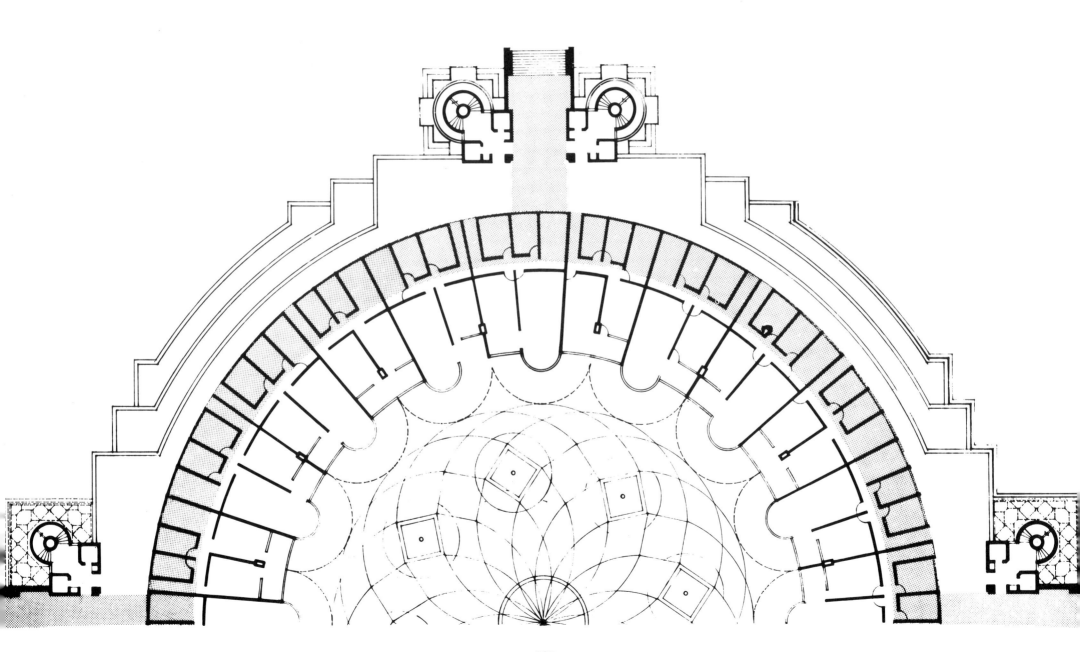

Time

'Li Kūlli ajalin Miad.'
(Every life-span has its appointed time.)

Hadith Sharif

Contemporary architects in the Islamic world have tried to embody Islamic values by including traditional architectural details on both the exterior and the interior of buildings on a scale which, due to the high costs of producing such traditional details, invalidates the financial feasibility of the projects. It is important to take into consideration the relationship which exists between shape and time and relate this to a human scale; thus, the floor heights and floor areas can be seen to be different. One can use traditional elements to serve different functions in order to give unity to the texture of the urban structure, whilst retaining a human scale. This could be achieved by enlarging or reducing these elements to take on a different function and at the same time have symbolic meaning. For example, **one can make use of the gateway concept to show a concept of axis, or use the column at a different scale to take a stairway or lift or use the patios instead of the thick walls which are not really needed in contemporary buildings.**

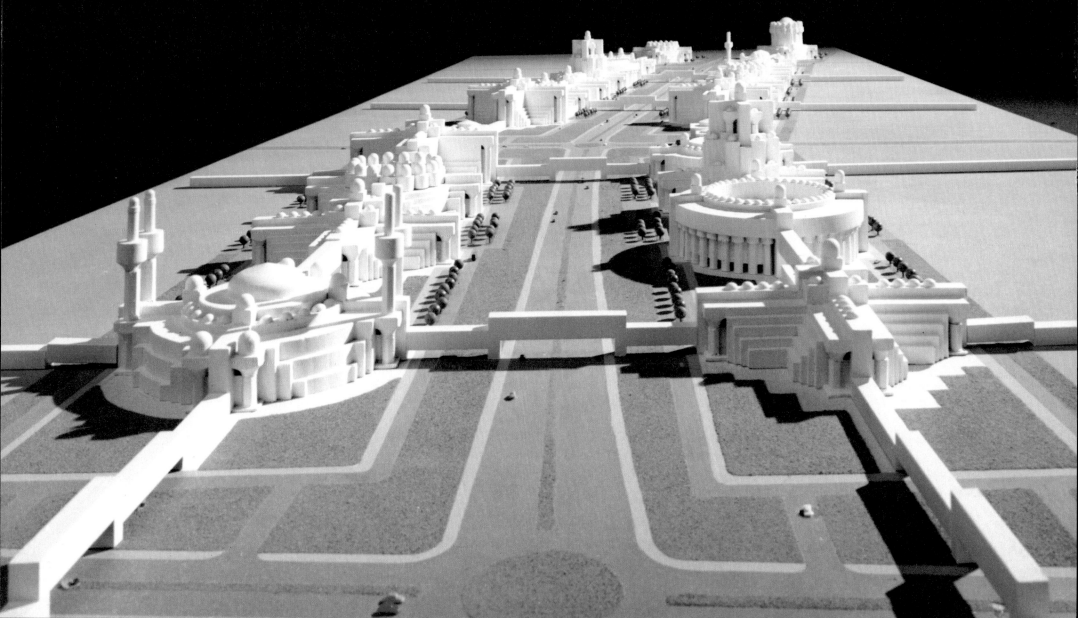

Strength

Capitals from the East

'Inna'l Laha ḥuwa'r Razzaqū dhu'l qūwwati'l Matin.'
(Indeed, Allah, is the One who gives livelihood, the Lord of unbreakable might.)

Quran (Al-Thariyyat 51:58)

'Afala yanẓūrūna ila'l-ibili kayfā khūliqat wa ila' sam'i Kayfā ruf'at wa ila'l-gibalī kayfa nuṣibat?'
(Do they not see how the camels were created, how the heavens were elevated, and how the mountains were erected?)

Quran (Al-Ghashiya 88:17–1)

'Don't think that glory is mere drink and a singing girl, glory lies in the sword and its unmatched smile.'

Al-Mutanabbi

Architecture of the Islamic world should reflect the relationship between man and his creator. (It is God who has elevated the skies and it is in his power to do so.) In Islamic architecture the connection between the building and the ground is important. Different bases have been used to give the observer a feeling of security. **The buildings appear as though they have actually been built by man, and are being supported by the earth, giving them a sense of strength without any element of optical illusion. Pillars and arches should be stressed to give a sense of strength** and, in addition, give the building the impression of having its roof on the earth and not just floating in the air, as exemplified by some of the Western architecture.

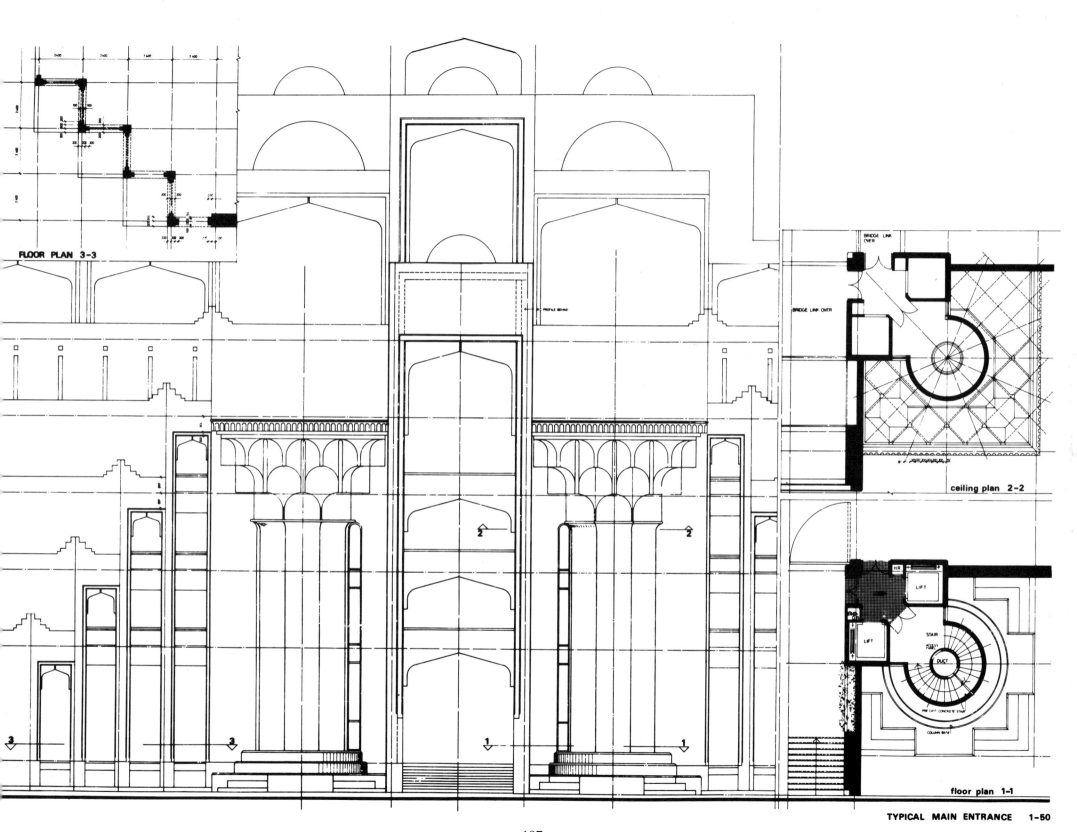

FLOOR PLAN 3-3

ceiling plan 2-2

floor plan 1-1

TYPICAL MAIN ENTRANCE   1-50

Interior of a Mosque (Ernst)

Heights

'Wā rafa'na lāka dhikrak.'
(We have elevated your fame.)

Quran (Yousif 12:100)

'Wa idha sakatta fa-'anta ablaghu khatibin galamun laka't-takhadha'l-anāmila minbarā.'
(And if you maintain silence, then the most eloquent preacher is the pen that chooses your finger for its pulpit.)
Al-Mutanabbi

Almost every ancient Islamic urban centre was dominated by its citadel. The relationship between the light and mercy is an old notion and from this idea the 'Mountain of Mercy' (*Jabil Al Rhma*) emerged. The mountain symbol is used to indicate the place of honour as in the Zigorates and pyramids in pre-Islamic days. High places were also used in places like schools. **The placing of living units in a high position is important, in order that there should be a feeling of security; each unit having a sense of being part of the earth and not merely being suspended in the air.** The earth in this case grants calm and mercy. The different storeys of the building must be graded so that each storey has ground in front of it. The concept of security, calm and mercy is a unifying factor in the design of the community.

Bab El Foutouh

Gateway

'Wa'tu'l būyūta min abwabihā.'
(Enter the house by the gates thereof.)

Quran (Al-Bagara 2:189)

'I turn my face away so that I do not see [your house].
But all of a sudden I find myself knocking at your door.'

Mohammad Riza ash-Shabibi

The purpose of the door was to hinder vandalism and to provide defence, but through the years man has become urbanized. With the advent of Islam, love and fraternity spread in conjunction with the defensive wars and campaigns. Architects were employed to design city gates, and with the spread of this new religion, gates assumed a fresh significance. Islam not only made use of the gateway politically, but some were also constructed in an artistic manner. There were several gates in every Islamic city and they were symbols of wonderful architecture. The gateway is an important structure, therefore it should be incorporated into the design of the new urban structure of Islamic cities. **The urban structure could be divided into different sections, each section having its own gateway to represent the symbol of unity.**

Bab El Nasr

Opening

Openings in Islamic architecture have their own special characteristics and differ according to the local style of architecture. The openings are based on the principles of a circle's interaction and connection. **The circle is the unifying principle of forming these openings and can be used in designing contemporary architecture for the Islamic world.**

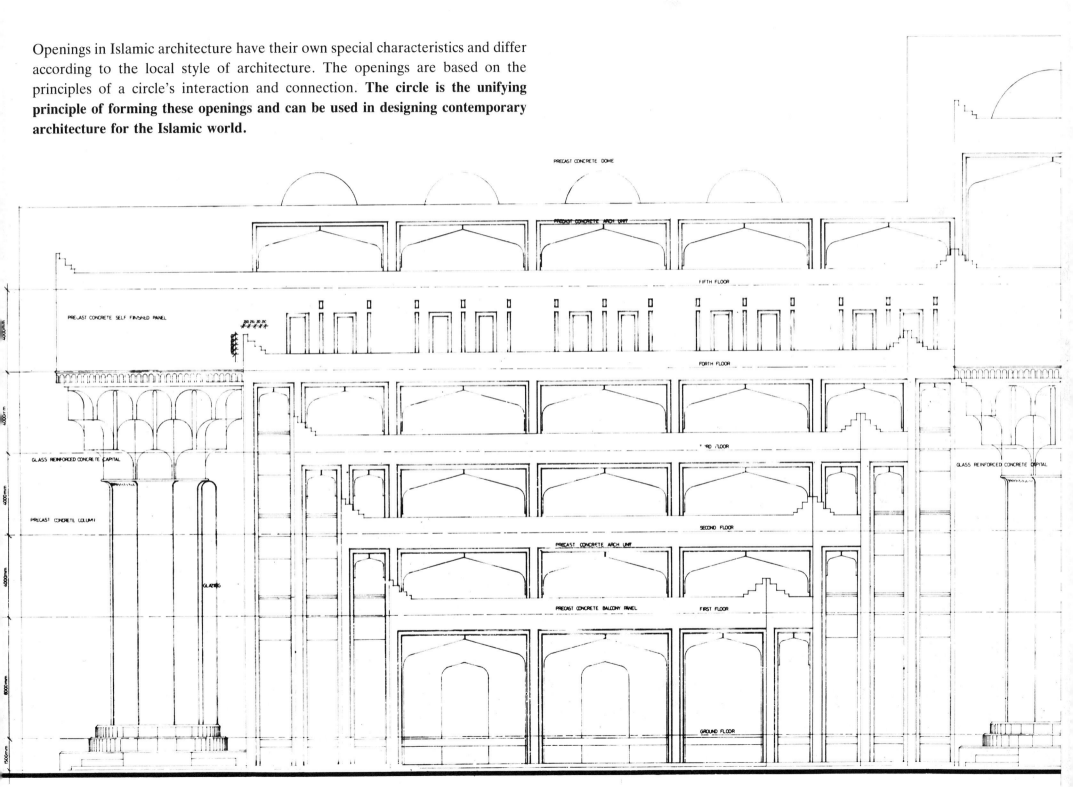

PRECAST CONCRETE DOME

PRECAST CONCRETE ARCH UNIT

FIFTH FLOOR

PRECAST CONCRETE SELF FINISHED PANEL

FORTH FLOOR

GLASS REINFORCED CONCRETE CAPITAL

THIRD FLOOR

GLASS REINFORCED CONCRETE CAPITAL

PRECAST CONCRETE COLUMN

SECOND FLOOR

PRECAST CONCRETE ARCH UNIT

GLAZING

PRECAST CONCRETE BALCONY PANEL

FIRST FLOOR

GROUND FLOOR

PART ELEVATION   1:50

Intermediate Space

'Qala lā tathriba 'alaikūmū'l-yawma yaghfirū'l-Lahū Lakūm wa Hūwā arḥamūi'r-Raḥimin.'

Quran (Yousif 12:92)

'A'la'l-mamāliki ma't-tafahumu ussuhu.
Wa'l-'adlu filu ha'itun wa di'a mu.'
(For no edifice survives on points of swords.
The loftiest states are those based on mutual understanding.)

Ahmad Shawqi

Architectural spaces in the Arabic city were made up of three parts: the positive space, which contains the operative functions, the negative space which contains the open courtyards and the intermediate space which is half open and is situated between the other two spaces. Such a space is called *Tarma*; **it links the two spaces giving the effect of unity.** This sort of space in the design of the architectural spaces is important in serving climatic purposes, in assisting the air circulation and also as an extension of the architectural space. **The extension in this case gives a feeling of security.**

Intermediate Spaces – Abbasid Period

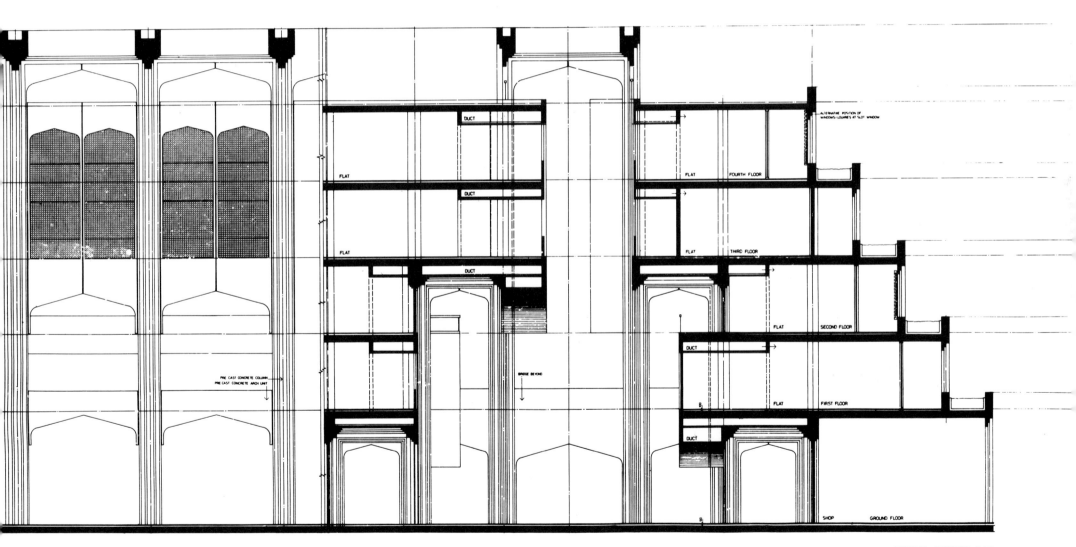

ALTERNATIVE POSITION OF
WINDOWS/LOUVRES AT SLOT WINDOW

DUCT

FLAT

DUCT   FLAT   FOURTH FLOOR

FLAT

FLAT   THIRD FLOOR

DUCT

FLAT   SECOND FLOOR

DUCT

PRE CAST CONCRETE COLUMN   BRIDGE BEYOND
PRE CAST CONCRETE ARCH UNIT   FLAT   FIRST FLOOR

DUCT

SHOP   GROUND FLOOR

TYPICAL SECTION 1:50

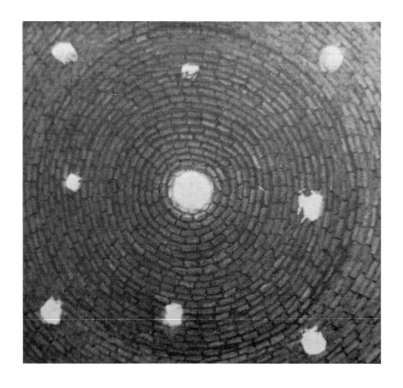

Dome

'Innama yakhsha'l Laha min 'ibadihi'l 'ulama'u.'
(The erudite among His bondment fear Allah alone.)
Quran (fatir 35:28)

Architectural elements have special characteristics in the Islamic world. Such elements are vaults and domes. **The dome plays an important part in representing the unity of space. It appears in Mosques, Madrassas and many other places** in different forms: such as half-domes, elongated domes and chequered domes. A main dome is raised in the middle section of the principal building and is surrounded by secondary domes. The use of pendentives helps create a smooth transition to the circle, from the square space on which the lower edges of the domes are based. **It is possible to use this dome in our present building alongside the use of modern building materials because of their great adaptability, and in so doing, to give the architecture of many types of buildings the same characteristics.**

Perforated domes

Aesthetics

Circular pattern calligraphy—G. Alani

'Inna'l Lāhā jamilūn yūhibbū'l jamal.'
(God is beautiful and loves beauty.)

Hadith Sharif

'Sūnī jamā laki 'annā innanā basharun
mina't turabi wa hadha'l-husnu rūhānī.'
(Guard your beauty from us,
For we are only mortals made of dust, and this beauty is
celestial.)

Ismail Sabri Basha

Islam did not differentiate between aesthetics and function
but tried to treat them as one element, the one comp-
lementing the other. Decoration in Islamic architecture
serves several functions; its purpose is to conceal the structure
rather than to reveal it. Calligraphy, geometrical pattern and
foliation can be used to give effect and make the space
function more pleasantly. Other elements which improve the
quality of the space, for example **the play of light on domes
and other spaces give more beauty to the space and unify the
interior and exterior.**

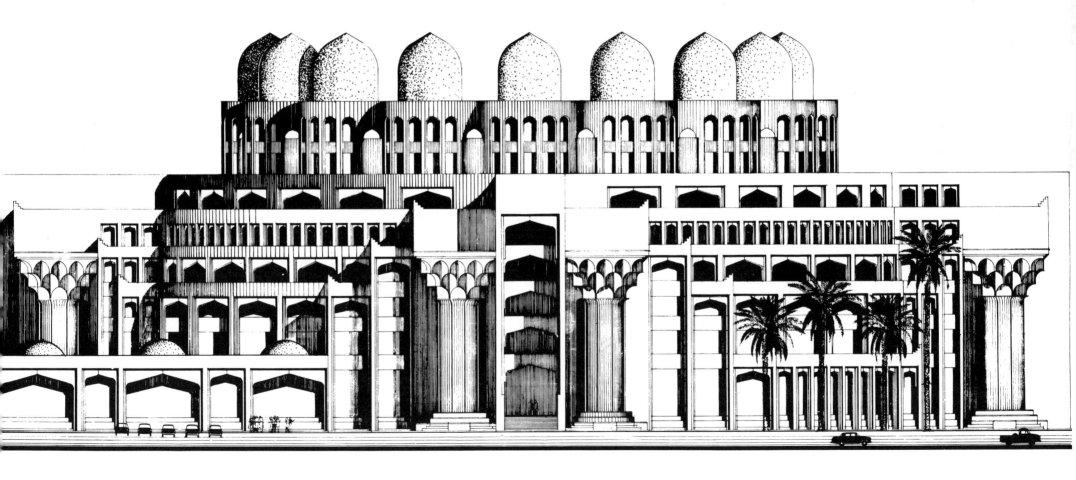

Residential units وحــدات سكنية

Fire

'*Allahu nūrū's samawati wa'l arḍi.*'
(God is the light of the heavens and earth.)

Hadith Sharif

'*Taksibu'sh-shamsu minka'n-nūra tāli'atan*
Ka-ma yaksibu minhā nūrahu'l-qamaru.'
(The rising sun owes its light to you.
Just as the moon owes its light to the sun.)

Al-Mutanabbi

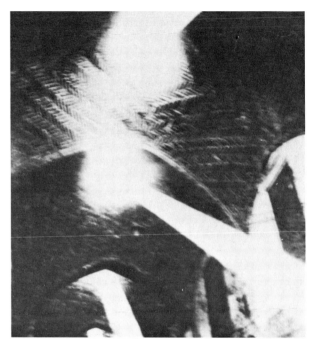

When one talks about fire, in the context of building, one means the heat and the light; the sunlight is essential in buildings which should remain unaffected by its heat. The problem is overcome by using cantilevered upper floors giving protection to the pedestrian while, at the same time, providing light.

Daylighting of bazaar by shafts of sunlight through holes in the apex of the domes.

Other examples can be found in domes perforated so that light passes through them indirectly, and the employment of the intermediate space (*Tarma*) between the outer and the inner space. This helps to lessen the impact of both light and heat at the same time. **The design of the building can treat the light and heat as a focal element in order to achieve unity.**

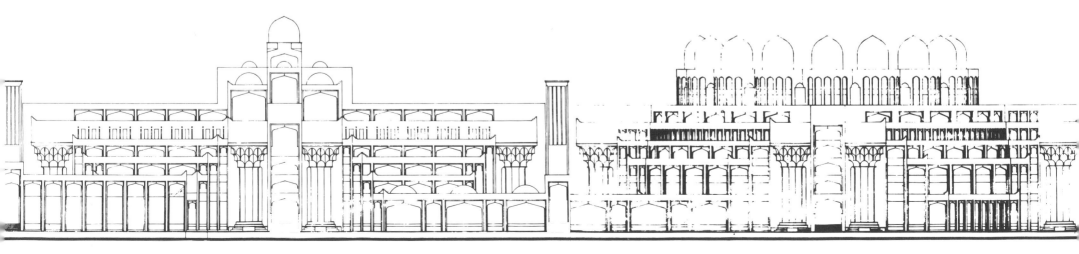

Air

'Fā-sakhkhrna lahu'r-riḥā tajri bī-amrihi rukha'an.'

Quran (Abrahim 14:18)

'Nasaja'r-rīhu 'ala'l-mā'i zarad
yā lahu dir'an manī'an law jamad.'

(The breeze has engraved a coat on the surface of the water. What a protective armoury it would be, if it only materializes.)

Al Mu Tamid Ben Abad

The atmospheric factors governing the area in which the Muslim Arab cities appear are very important. Of particular importance is the wind which helps to ventilate the architectural spaces. Structures can be created to direct air movement and at the same time, **they can give an architectural texture to the urban structure and a unifying characteristic to the city.** Such forms are wind catchers, wind towers and perforated domes.

Wind tower (Al Badgir)

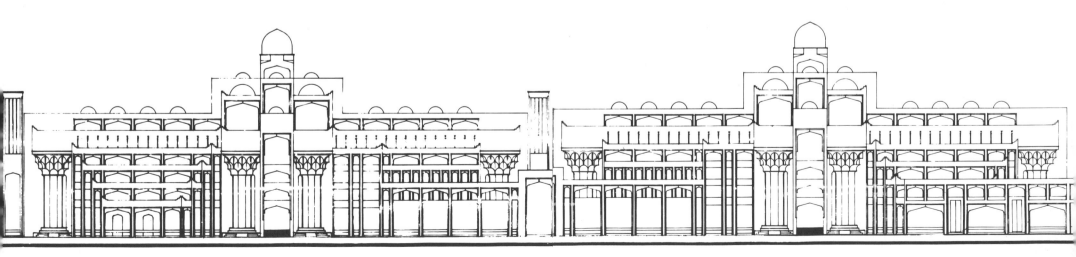

Earth

'Wā idha qila lūhūm lā tūfsidū fi'l arḍi qalū innama naḥnū muṣliḥūn.'
(And when it is said to them: make not mischief in the earth, they say: we are peacemakers only.)

Quran (Al-Baqara 2:11)

'Man originated from the earth and will return to it.'

This fact acknowledges man's relationship with the earth. In Islamic religion the daily prayers in which man's forehead touches the earth represent the relationship between man and earth. The shape of the earth affects the urban structure through its topographical and geological make-up. For example, **the desert towns are inwardly open and the mountain towns are outwardly open. Such facts as these are important in creating a base for unity in the urban structure.**

Earth formation

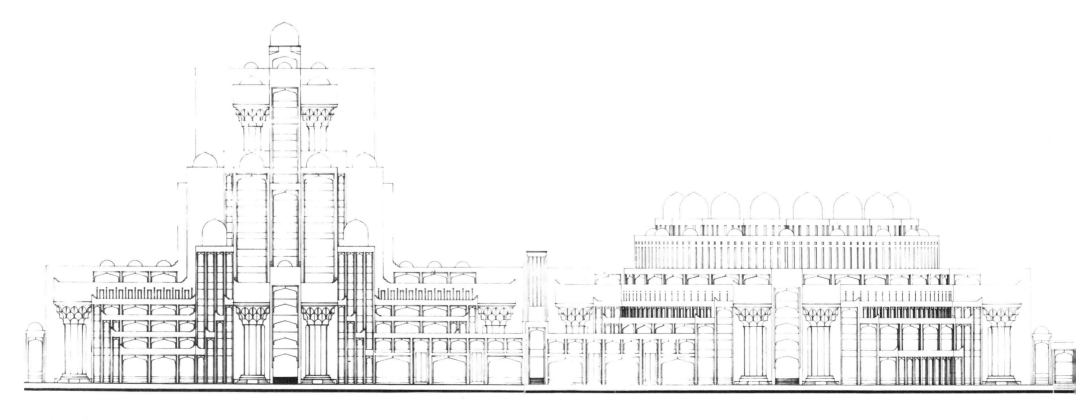

Water

'Wā ja'alna mina'l-ma'ī kulla s̲hay'in hayyin.'
(We made every living thing from water.)

Quran (Al-Anbia 21:30)

The Muslims were the first to use the science of water pressure. They managed to bring water from the wells to the Mosques for ablutions using a very ingenious method. **In design, water is like a magnet which polarizes space. Where there are open spaces in the Muslim urban structure water can be a focal point.** It represents the meaning of unity and also *Al-Rahma* (Mercy). In addition, it makes the atmosphere more pleasant.

Circular pattern—water cisterns

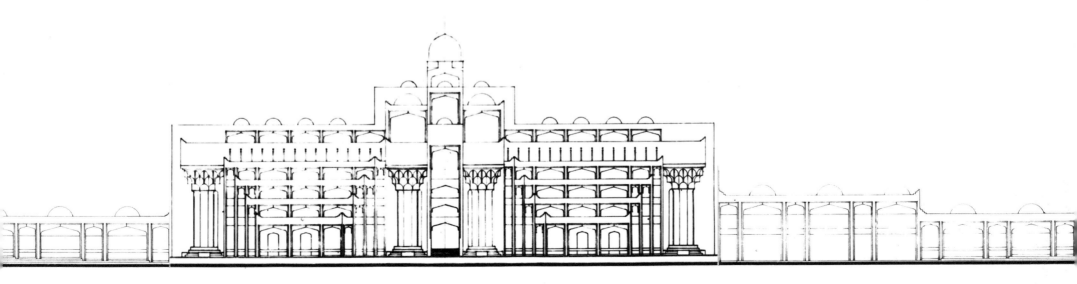

Community

عَنْ أَبِي عَبْدِ الرَّحْمٰنِ عَبْدِ اللهِ بْنِ عُمَرَ بْنِ الْخَطَّابِ رَضِيَ اللهُ عَنْهُمَا

قَالَ : سَمِعْتُ رَسُولَ اللهِ صَلَّى اللهُ عَلَيْهِ وَسَلَّمَ يَقُولُ :

« بُنِيَ الْإِسْلَامُ عَلَى خَمْسٍ : شَهَادَةِ أَنْ لَا

إِلٰهَ إِلَّا اللهُ وَأَنَّ مُحَمَّداً رَسُولُ اللهِ ، وَإِقَامِ

الصَّلَاةِ ، وَإِيتَاءِ الزَّكَاةِ ، وَحَجِّ الْبَيْتِ ، وَصَوْمِ

رَمَضَانَ » .

رَوَاهُ الْبُخَارِيُّ وَمُسْلِمٌ .

On the authority of Abū 'Abd ar-Raḥman 'Abdullah, the son of 'Umar ibn al-Khaṭṭāb (may Allah be pleased with them both), who said: I heard the Messenger of Allah (may the blessings and peace of Allah be upon him) say:

Islam has been built on five [pillars]: testifying that there is no god but Allah and that Muḥammad is the Messenger of Allah, performing the prayers, paying the *zakāt*, making the pilgrimage to the House, and fasting in Ramaḍān.

It was related by al-Bukhārī and Muslim.

The design of the Muslim community must encourage all those who live in it to live a proper Islamic life according to the Divine Law. **The creation of a modern urban structure should not only be based on bricks and concrete, but equally should show humanitarian consideration for Islamic principles and values.** Islam says that the community should be like a family, and this should also be a basis for building the city. The relationship of the individual to Islamic law is achieved through one's behaviour and the fulfilment of one's role within society, which can only become complete through the link with the architectural environment which surrounds the community both financially and morally.

Typical pedestrian route

Movement

'Al-'Ajalatū mina'sh-shaiṭān wa'l ta'anni mina'r Raḥman.'
(Impatience comes from the devil, whilst patience comes from God.)

Hadith Sharif

'Rijlāhu rijlun wa'l-yadāni yadun
Wa fi'luhu mā turidu'l-kaffu wa'l-qadamu.'
([My horse is so swift] that both its hind legs become one, and its front feet become one straight line. And it does what the hand and foot of its rider desire.)

Al-Mutanabbi

The original Islamic Arab city was a pedestrian city. The design of the modern city is affected by measurements relating to the flow of traffic. To give the city a sense of humanity it is necessary to find a way to relate human movement and the movement of the car. There are three types of vehicular systems which could achieve such an environment. Firstly, the creation of peripheral roads used solely for high speed driving; secondly, further peripheral roads used for short journeys; and thirdly, slow roads which would form part of the architectural space. **This type of grading in the scale of movement can achieve both the humanitarian environment of the old Islamic city and meet with the modern requirements of man in the contemporary city.** In the case of the pedestrian, one could suggest a system which would **connect the whole community by using corridors of semi-covered pathways,** separated from the cars and using bridges at the crossing points. The vertical separation allows for the location of parking areas in a covered structure; a more preferable system in the 'hot' area, where pedestrian and vehicular systems meet. One can also locate services such as petrol stations near the vehicular system and restaurants and cafés near the pedestrian system.

Thus the path which serves man and his machine can pass through the whole community and serve the architectural spaces. It would also be possible to travel from one point to another by car within the shortest possible distance, and pedestrians could walk throughout the whole community, which would give them a sense of security and serenity.

Crossing

'Show us the straight path, the path of those whom you have favoured.'

Quran (1:6–7)

'As-safarqiṭ'atūn mina'ṣ ṣaqar.'
(Travelling is hellish.)

Hadith Sharif

'Amira'l Mu'minīna ra'aitu jisran
amurru 'ala's-Sirāti wa lā 'alaili.'
(Commander of the faithful I have seen a bridge
I would rather shun for the narrow and dangerous pathway separating Hell from
Heaven.)

Ahmed Shawqi

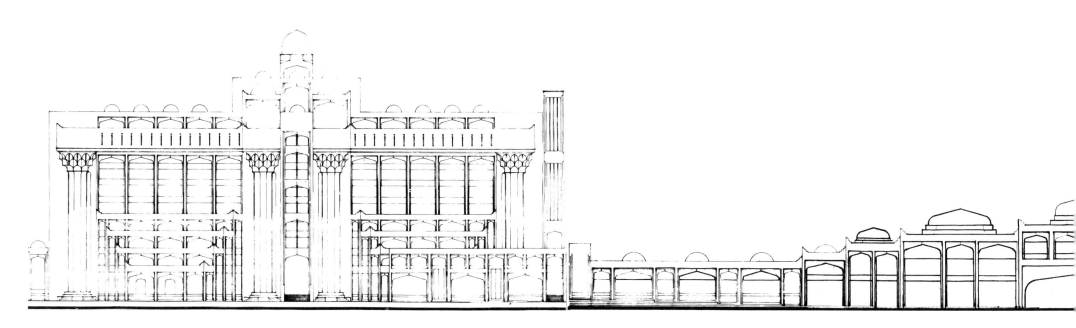

In Islamic architecture, where there were mountains and water to be crossed, bridges of architectural significance were erected. Examples of these are Koprucay Bridge, Jampur Bridge, Khuajau Bridge. In the case of the Jampur Bridge, a pavilion was added later for tea-houses and in time it became the venue for a market at Khwju Bridge at Isfahan. The central roadway is flanked by arcaded galleries used for walking, standing and chatting. Every part of the community should stimulate activity in order to achieve unity; **activities are an important element in unifying the spaces within the urban structure**. Where crossings are necessary within modern urban structures, activities can be located on the different levels such as petrol stations, car parks, restaurants, cafés and entertainment places.

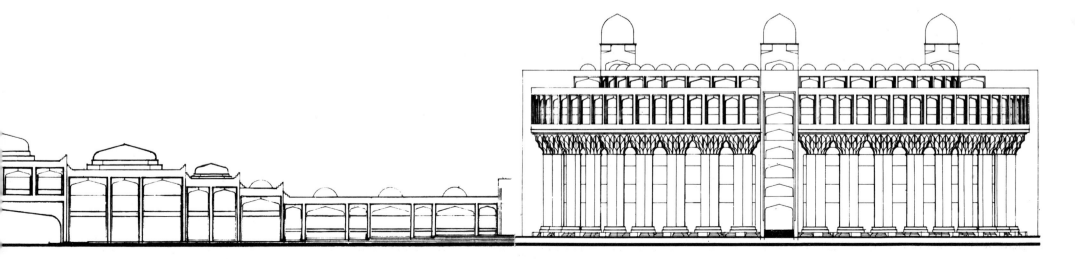

The Holy Rock (C. Haag)

Religion

'Lakūm dirūkūm wa liya din.'
(Unto you your religion and unto me my religion.)
Quran (Al-Kafiroun 109:6)

'Aghāyātu'd-dini'an tahfu shawāribakum
yā'ummatan dahikat min Jahliha'l-umamu.'
(Is the aim of religion shaving off your whiskers
O nation that has made itself the laughing stock of the world?)
Al-Mutanabbi

The Mosque is considered to be the spiritual and cultural centre of the Arabic-Islamic cities. It has the place of honour in the town. **Round it the natural urban structure grows.** It was the nucleus and the centre of Islamic teachings and the venue of the government and the governed—the status of the Mosque in the city expresses the extent of the people's adherence to the Islamic faith as a religion and as a system of life.

Housing

'There was indeed a sign for Sheba in the dwelling place: two gardens on the right hand and the left. Eat of the provision of your God and never render thanks to him. A fair land and an indulgent Lord!'

Quran (Saba 43:15)

'Masākinu Jinnatin law sāra fihā
Sulaimanun la-sāra bi-turjumāni.'

(They are like the dwellings of jin
if the [multi-linguist] Solomon happened to be there,
He would require an interpreter.)

Al-Mutanabbi

'Oh guest, should you visit us, you would find us the guests and you the Master of the House.'

Mustatraf

The Arab name *Masakin,* meaning homes or home, is related to the word *sakina*—peaceful and holy. The living unit of a Muslim should have two types of space; private and public. The most fundamental division occurs between male reception areas and the family living area where the family work and relax. The plan of the living unit should be such that guests can be entertained without interfering with family life. In order that Islamic living units provide privacy, the planning must accommodate double circulation, thus achieving direct entry. **In the living unit most spaces are not functionally specific, the rooms can be interchanged for sleeping and eating. Such flexibility reflects the concept of unity within the living unit. The most important factor to be considered in designing the living units are the people themselves.** The preliminary design should take on a form which can adapt and accept changes after a more comprehensive study of the behavioural patterns of the types of people who inhabit the units.

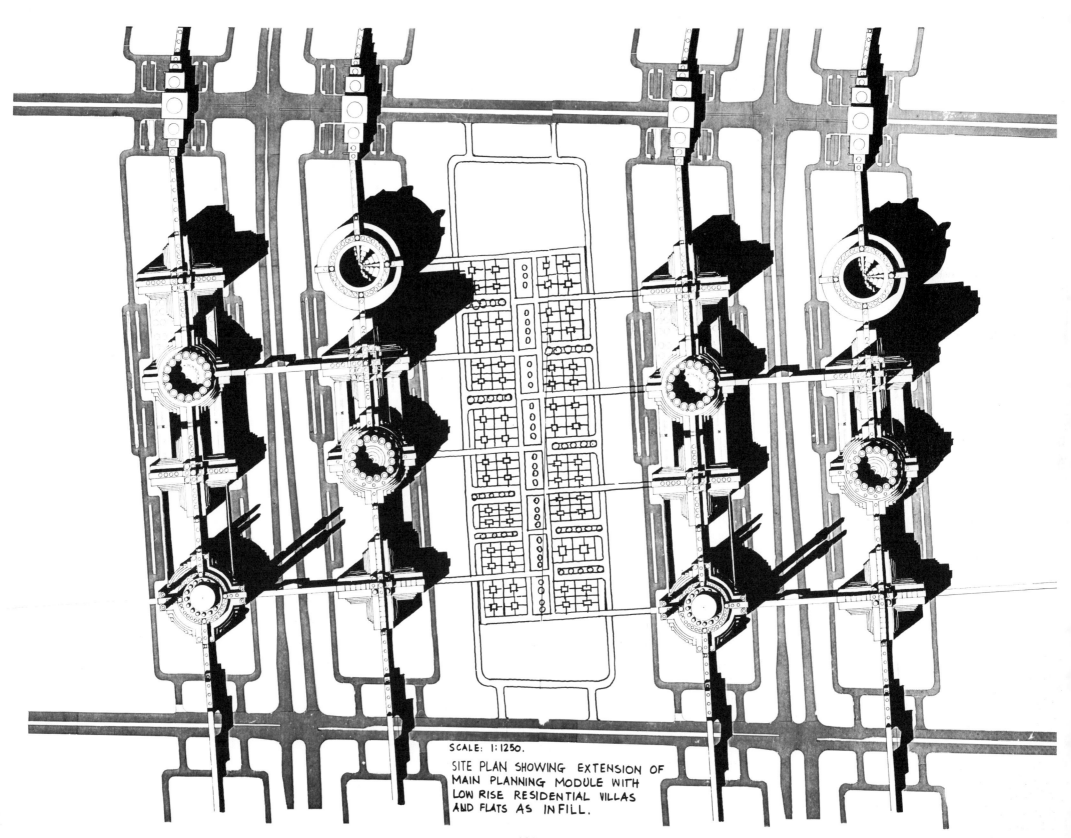

SCALE: 1:1250.

SITE PLAN SHOWING EXTENSION OF
MAIN PLANNING MODULE WITH
LOW RISE RESIDENTIAL VILLAS
AND FLATS AS INFILL.

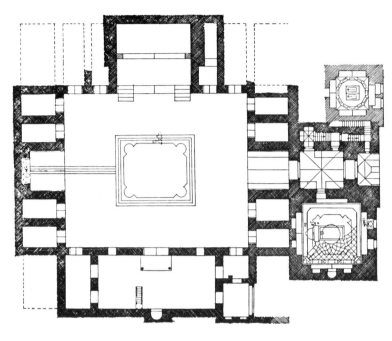

Madrassa al-Nuriya al-Kubra, Damascus

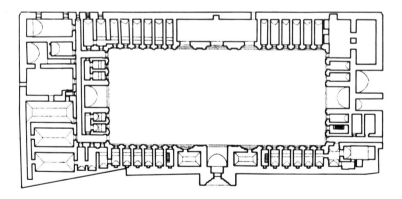

Madrassa Mustansiriya, Baghdad

Education

'Innama yakhsha'l Laha min 'ibadihi'l 'ulama'u.'
(The erudite among His bondment fear Allah alone.)
Quran (fatir 35:28)

The first Arab teacher in Islam was the prophet Mohammed. The first book the prophet taught was the Quran and the first building used in teaching in Islam was the Mosque. In this context it is of importance in the planning of our urban structure that the location of the places of education should be related to the places of worship. **It is like knowledge and faith: they complement each other. Schools (Madrassas), Libraries (Maktaba) and Mosques (Masjid) should be integrated together in the Islamic way of life,** containing a place for worshipping God, a place for teaching the Quran, clinics for emergencies, food and drink, residences for students and a central courtyard with water to create a pleasant environment. This should also be connected with other facilities in the community, such as markets and main meeting areas, so that it becomes part of it. It should be one part of a whole, creating unity in the urban structure.

Al Mualim

Cleanliness

'Al-Naẓafah min āl īmān.'
(Cleanliness is part of the faith.)

Hadith Sharif

The call to make the contemporary Islamic urban structure more closely related to its origins does not only depend on making use of the traditional architecture and its artistic values, but also on planning from a humanitarian viewpoint. One of the most important elements is the provision of necessary requirements for comfortable living, such as baths (*hammams*) and facilities for washing which is a very important part of a Muslim's daily life. **Cleanliness is a concept that should be adopted throughout the whole community to act as a unifying factor.**

Hammam—late Islamic period

136

Health

'Inna li-jasadika 'alaika ḥaqqūn'.
(You have a duty towards your body.)

Hadith Sharif

'Yamūtu rā'i'd-da'ni fi da'inhī
mitata Jālinosa fī tibbihi.'
(A shepherd dies amidst his flock
Like the death of Galen amidst his medical knowledge.)

Al-Mutanabbi

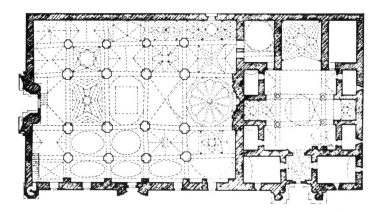

Divrig Hospital

Mustashfa in Arabic is a place where healing (*shafaa*) is sought. Places of *shafaa* should be characterized by cleanliness. They should be planned carefully to take care of the elderly, following the injunction of the Holy Quran: '*O Lord, have mercy on them fast as they had mercy on me in my childhood [ch 'al-Isra].*' **The Islamic urban structure should incorporate within it many of these places.** They should form part of the other units in accordance with the principle of unity, as, for example, a clinic containing pharmacies. Such places should be planned to look very pleasant with courtyards and fountains. They should have many separate sections, and be provided with a radio system to recite verses of the Quran in the morning and music in the evening and also equipped to supply food. **Such things make the patient feel at home in this environment and also unify the place of healing and the place of living with the whole community.**

137

Hospitality

'Qula inna ha'ūla'i ḍaifi fa-lā tafḍaḥūn.'
(He said these are my guests, so do not embarrass me in front of them.)

Quran (Al-Hagar 15:68)

'Sakantu'l-khana fi baladī ka'annī
alehu safarin taqadhafuhu'd-durubu.'
(I dwell in an inn in my own homeland
Like a travelling vagabond. Moving from one road to another.)

Rusafi

Hotels/resting places were first found located in Islam: in the rural areas the *caravanserai* appear as distinguished architectural monuments. In the urban areas, a *Khan* was essentially a warehouse with different apartments on the upper floors. In the modern urban structure, the hotel is replacing these types of buildings. Today in all modern Islamic cities hotels appear. Because of the different life-styles people lead, these hotels require different types of planning. **One has to study cultural behaviour and design accordingly; for example, families stay together whilst travelling therefore the planning of such a building should be flexible in order to accommodate these demands. Hospitality is the main Islamic principle which acts as a unifying factor in design.**

Protection

'Mā ja'ala' lahu min bahiratin wa la sa'ibatin wā lā waṣilatīn wā la ḥamin.'
(God has not appointed anything in the nature of sacred camels with slit ears or those going at random, or joining their brothers or protecting their backs from carrying burdens.)
Quran (Al-Maida 5:103)

'If the words of history were written without being influenced by the sword, a thousand walls would fall.'

Forts and walls originally appeared in Islamic architecture for defensive purposes and were decorated with distinctive patterns which gave them a character of their own. This type of architecture is the most direct expression of power in designing a new urban structure. **By adopting a particular style, buildings such as police stations and guard houses can assume the characteristics of protection and power.** Such a style can be taken from the traditional architecture of the area to link the present unity with the past.

139

The Palace, Abu Dhabi

Garden

'Fa'anbātnā fihā habbā, wa 'inaban wa gadba, wa zaitūnan wa na<u>kh</u>la, wa ḥada'iqa <u>g</u>hulba.'
(We caused the grain to grow therein, and grapes and green fodder and olive trees and palm trees and garden-closes of thick foliage.)

Quran (Abs 80:27–30)

'Maghani'<u>sh-sh</u>i'bi tīban fi'l maqhāni,
bi-manzilati'r-rabi'i mina'z-zamāni.
(The gardens of the ravine of Bawwan, compared with others in beauty are like springtime compared to other seasons of the year.)

Al-Mutanabbi

According to the Islamic principles, the design concept of the garden is composed of independent space which has its own pattern. The garden is an enclosed space just like a man's body which encloses the soul. The plan of the garden for example can have a courtyard with a central pavilion surrounded by a geometrical pattern of trees or it can have a basin of water with a fountain in the centre. This type of planning generates a centripetal force and can be used in all types of buildings thereby achieving unity in the whole urban structure.

The trees, flowers and plantations are very much more important. For example, palm trees have always been significant in the life of the Muslim (**the name of Al Nakhlah is repeated in many suras in the Quran and in many sacred sayings of the prophet Mohammed:** *'God's blessing be upon him'*); it is therefore very important to use such trees in planning to unify the green appearance throughout the community.

Al Nakhlah palm tree

References:

1 The Holy Quran

2 Hadith Sharif